THE EVALUATOR AND MANAGEMENT

Volume 4
SAGE RESEARCH PROGRESS SERIES IN EVALUATION

SAGE RESEARCH PROGRESS SERIES IN EVALUATION

SAGE RESEARCH PROGRESS SERIES IN EVALUATION
Volume 4

Edited by
HERBERT C. SCHULBERG
and
JEANETTE M. JERRELL

THE
EVALUATOR
AND
MANAGEMENT

Published in cooperation with the
EVALUATION RESEARCH SOCIETY

SAGE PUBLICATIONS   Beverly Hills   London

Copyright © 1979 by Sage Publications, Inc.

For information address:

SAGE Publications, Inc.
275 South Beverly Drive
Beverly Hills, California 90212

SAGE Publications Ltd
28 Banner Street
London EC1Y 8QE, England

Printed in the United States of America

Library of Congress Cataloging in Publication Data
Main entry under title:

The evaluator and management.

(Sage research progress series in evaluation; v. 4)
Bibliography: p.
1. Evaluation research (Social action program)—
Addresses, essays, lectures. I. Schulberg, Herbert C.
II. Jerrell, Jeanette. III. Series.
H62.E86   309.1'73'092   79-19458
ISBN 0-8039-1304-4
ISBN 0-8039-1305-2 pbk.

FIRST PRINTING

Contents

ABOUT THIS SERIES

The SAGE RESEARCH PROGRESS SERIES IN EVALUATION is a series of concisely edited works designed to present notable, previously unpublished writing on topics of current concern to the evaluation community. In keeping with a vision of evaluation as a methodological enterprise with outcomes at both the policy-making and services delivery levels, the series is designed to present state-of-the-art volumes for use by instructors and students of evaluation, researchers, practitioners, policy-makers, and program administrators.

Each volume (4 to 6 new titles will be published in each calendar year) focuses on themes which emerge from the previous year's annual meeting of the Evaluation Research Society—revised and supplemented by specially commissioned works.

The series begins in 1979 with five volumes, largely selected from papers delivered at the 2nd Annual Meeting of the Evaluation Research Society held in Washington, D.C. on November 2-4, 1978. The volumes in this inaugural year include:

*QUALITATIVE AND QUANTITATIVE METHODS IN EVALUATION RESEARCH, edited by Thomas D. Cook and Charles S. Reichardt

*EVALUATOR INTERVENTIONS: Pros and Cons, edited by Robert Perloff

*TRANSLATING EVALUATION INTO POLICY, edited by Robert F. Rich

*THE EVALUATOR AND MANAGEMENT, edited by Herbert C. Schulberg and Jeanette M. Jerrell

*EVALUATION IN LEGISLATION, edited by Franklin M. Zweig

We are pleased that these initial volumes in the *SAGE RESEARCH PROGRESS SERIES IN EVALUATION* so well represent significant interdisciplinary contributions to the literature. Comments and suggestions from our readers will be welcomed.

SERIES EDITORS:

Susan E. Salasin, National Institute of Mental Health
Robert Perloff, University of Pittsburgh

1

Herbert C. Schulberg
Jeanette M. Jerrell
University of Pittsburgh
School of Medicine

PROMISES AND PITFALLS IN THE EVALUATOR'S AND MANAGER'S PURSUIT OF ORGANIZATIONAL EFFECTIVENESS

Program evaluation has matured in the past two decades from pious declarations about the need to assess organizational effectiveness to a major field of activity and professional specialization. Stimulated by growing pressures for accountability and diminishing resources, program managers have been forced to employ administrative and assessment procedures satisfactory to internal and/or external auditors. Program evaluation thus has come to be viewed as an integral component of managerial functions and responsibilities (Attkisson et al., 1978; Binner, 1975).

Not surprisingly, the growing variety of evaluations completed during the past years has spurred growing interest in the utility of these efforts. The assumption has been made that evaluation findings, particularly those revealing negative or insignificant programmatic consequences, should necessarily produce organizational change. However, the literature of recent years is replete with equivocal reports regarding the impact of evaluation data on the programs being studied. This has led many to reach a nihilistic conclusion about evaluation's utility. Fortunately, others are more optimistic and they have seized upon this dubious state of affairs to emphasize the need for better understanding of the multifaceted process whereby research influences policy. The more sanguine observers are urging, in particular, that empirical investigations focus upon the factors abetting and constraining the utilization process. The original papers included in this volume consider the utilization process from both conceptual and pragmatic perspectives, and their contributions to this analysis will be highlighted in the latter part of our overview.

UTILIZATION AS A DEPENDENT VARIABLE

As program evaluation has burgeoned into the major enterprise it presently is, metaevaluations have become increasingly common. The evaluation of evaluations can scrutinize an assessment project from any of several perspectives during or after its completion (Cook and Gruder, 1978), but the criterion of utilization has attracted particular attention in determining an evaluation's worth. As early as the mid-1960s, Weiss (1966) exhorted evaluators to include among their concerns and empirical studies analyses of the factors affecting utilization of findings and the relative influence of data upon political decision-making. This exhortation was particularly apt, as various reports began to describe pessimistic conclusions regarding the low utility of evaluative findings to program administrators (Wholey et al., 1970; Rossi, 1971). Although subsequent studies have produced further illustrations of poorly utilized assessment data, depictions of how and when evaluation can affect administrative decisions also have emerged in recent years. Examples of these more positive illustrations are Lynn's (1972) analysis of HEW policy-making with regard to health care services and educational assistance programs and studies of evaluation's impact on community mental health center policy and practice (Beigel, 1974; Bigelow, 1975; Rossman et al., 1979).

With the emergence of negative, positive, and even inconsistent findings, we have come to recognize that research utilization is a far more complex process than had been initially conceived.

Therefore, metaevaluations in which utilization is the key dependent variable must be designed in a more thoughtful manner than was realized previously. For example, Weiss (1972) and Ciarlo (1974) found that it is crucial to select a proper time frame within which evaluation findings can be expected to have their impact; when the time frame was extended, utilization was found to increase. Patton's (1978) study found administrative decision-making to be cumulative in nature and to include both cognitive and affective elements. Thus, while evaluation findings did not produce an immediate and directly discernible impact upon program policy, the administrators studied by Patton acknowledged that these data were considered in their deliberations and reduced the ambiguity which they had been experiencing previously. A metaevaluation focused solely on policy change would not have detected these subtler impacts of the evaluation study.

Presently, it can be concluded that while there is general agreement that the manner in which evaluation results are utilized has important theoretical and practical implications, the critical parameters of the utilization process still warrant extensive study. Thus, until better clarification is achieved, metaevaluations using utilization as the key dependent variable are likely to produce findings whose meanings are difficult to interpret.

EVALUATION FINDINGS:
FACTORS AFFECTING THEIR UTILIZATION

As administrators, evaluators, and social scientists gain increasing awareness of the complexities inherent in the utilization process, a body of knowledge will develop about the multiple factors influencing this process. A comprehensive framework organizing and explicating the interrelationships of pertinent variables will be needed to link such diverse but relevant fields as research methodology, communication, knowledge dissemination, organizational development, and policy analysis. In anticipation of such an emergent conceptual schema, we will here employ that recently proposed by Attkisson et al. (1978) in their analysis of obstacles to evaluation's utilization. They suggest that (1) the validity of findings, (2) the utility of findings, (3) the pressure of negative findings for program justification, (4) program management deficiencies, and (5) the complexity of decision-making are central to the utilization process. Before reviewing these five dimensions, we will consider first the nature of human services organizations and the manager-evaluator relationships within them.

The Organizational Environment

In considering the gap between evaluation studies and their utilization, Schulberg et al. (1969) emphasized that managerial decisions to accept or reject proposed change occur in the context of complex social systems. There are key differences in the goals and operating procedures of those conducting research studies and those responsible for program development. The ideology of evaluative research, which supports the interpretation and communication of findings, may well conflict with certain organizational values. The latter frequently favor symbolic or ritualistic evaluation so that even when homage is paid by the organization to the theoretic merit of assessments, managers also routinely avoid substantive data emerging from these studies. Wildavsky (1979) notes that even organizations strongly committed to self-evaluation must assess selected activities whose outcome is sure to be positive so that essential environmental support will be maintained. Furthermore, Wildavsky stresses that evaluation can never be fully rewarded: other considerations often prevail in the decision-making process even when the "powers that be" would like to follow its dictates. A cogent review of other sociopolitical factors affecting evaluation research and its utilization is provided by Wilderman (1979).

This brief depiction of the organizational environment within which evaluation is conducted and communicated suggests that fundamental dilemmas exist in the evaluator-manager relationship. These dilemmas may manifest themselves in various ways and at different points in the evaluation process. Krause's (1978) analysis of the interdependence between managerial authority and evaluative expertise led him to conclude that only some facets of these two domains can coexist. Most of the others are antagonistic and inevitably will produce conflict of the type evident when managers consider the implications of evaluative data for service delivery. A related analysis by Windle and Neigher (1978) of the inherent tensions between managers and evaluators led them to distinguish the amelioration, accountability, and advocacy models of evaluation. The ethical dilemmas integral to each model are described by Windle and Neigher, with particular reference to the implications of each model for the evaluator's role in the utilization of findings.

A further basic issue with regard to evaluation's organizational environment is where in the organizational chart to place persons fulfilling this function. Attkisson and Hargreaves (1979) suggest that evaluators may function on a continuum which ranges from clerical/compilation tasks to leadership/integration activities. To be most effective in highlighting the implications of data for practice, the evaluator's role should be embedded in the organization's decision-making process at both the operational and long-range policy planning levels. The program evaluator optimally would be placed at the organization's hub, with prompt access to the most recent program data and direct responsibility to the organization's chief administrator. However, this coveted executive niche, which still is exceptional for evaluators, produces its own tensions and role conflicts. Evaluators must resolve the tensions if they are to successfully accomplish their goals for the utilization of data.

Validity of findings. A fundamental requirement of research methodology is that findings produced by a study must be germane to the questions being investigated. In performing evaluative research, however, this basic premise often creates profound problems. Among the dilemmas encountered in the design and conduct of valid evaluations are: (1) the difficulties of translating broadly stated programmatic goals into measurable objectives (Weiss, 1966); (2) the constantly changing nature of the program being evaluated (Binner, 1975; Weiss, 1966); (3) the inappropriateness of the experimental paradigm (Edwards et al., 1975; Nagi, 1976); (4) the lack of appropriate outcome measures (Weiss, 1966); (5) the dearth of adequately trained methodologists (Attkisson et al., 1978); and (6) the need for formative rather than summative data (Cohen, 1977). Issues of validity are most likely to be raised when evaluators generate negative findings about program effectiveness and suggest major changes in organizational structure and practice. Not surprisingly, less concern is exhibited about an evaluation's validity when it produces positive findings.

Utility of findings. The academic training of most evaluators orients them to issues of scientific validity, but the primary concern of program managers centers on the utility of data for needed administrative decisions. Weiss (1966), Binner (1975), Cox (1977), and Patton (1978) are among those who have emphasized the urgency of evaluators identifying a program's key decision makers and working actively and adaptively with these consumers of evaluative findings. While the evaluator's professional esteem and status may be predicated on competence in research design and instrumentation, usefulness to management is dependent on the desire and ability of the evaluator to work on the organizational issues pertinent to service delivery and continued survival.

The evaluator's commitment to maximize the utility of findings for programmatic practice has implications for choice of assessment model. Schulberg and Baker (1968) contrasted the goal attainment and systems models in relation to the implementation of findings. While the goal attainment model facilitates methodological rigor and enhances validity, the organizational objectives chosen for study may be insignificant ones. This model also fallaciously implies that specific goals can be evaluated and modified in isolation from other organizational goals. The system model is far more methodologically complex and expensive to perform. It does have the merit, however, of seeking to comprehend the organizational structure within which goals are pursued and the degree to which goals are achieved under given sets of circumstances. Furthermore, feedback requirements are integral to the system model so that structural linkages exist between the evaluator and manager, obviating the need to create ad hoc linkages for each new evaluation report.

Negative findings and program justification. Positive evaluations are interpreted as a justification for maintaining the status quo. Negative findings are perceived as reflecting adversely on the status quo and requiring programmatic change. The administrator's hesitance to act on findings of the latter type is exacerbated when the evaluation summarily rejects the program's worth (Rossi, 1971). The evaluator is cast as the bearer of sad tidings and is afforded pariah-like treatment. Nevertheless, the evaluator must abide by the data's implications and present options for the administrator's consideration. Weiss (1966) accepts the inevitability of organizational resistance to change and suggests that evaluators develop coalitions with such countervailing bodies as the political structure and funding sources.

Administrative deficiencies. Many of the individuals administering human service programs are clinicians who have assumed this role with little or no formal training in management. They tend to be particularly unfamiliar with procedures for generating, utilizing, and controlling the information sources pertinent to their program (Feldman, 1975) and have little knowledge of the complexities of applied research. Given this reality, evaluators must plan and conduct program assessments in ways that permit managers to learn about validity requirements and to become familiar with both the strengths and limitations of evaluative studies (Cohen, 1977; Cox, 1977; Weiss, 1966). Lacking formal training in administration and/or evaluation, managers seek prescriptions for organizational effectiveness and will underutilize or overgeneralize evaluation findings (Flanagan, 1976; Glock, 1976).

Horst et al. (1974) reviewed three related characteristics of human services administrators which tend to inhibit the utilization of evaluation results: (a) they may have unclear definitions of the problems to be addressed, the interventions to be undertaken, and the outcomes to be expected; (b) they may have unclear notions about the relationship between the program model and resource expenditures; and (c) they may lack the motivation and/ or the authority to act on evaluative results.

Complexity of decision-making. We had noted earlier that evaluators' inadequate conceptualization of organizational decision-making has hindered their ability to influence the process with evaluative findings. Rather than viewing organizational decision-making as a complex, multifaceted activity, evaluators have tended to consider it in a linear, unidimensional way (Attkisson et al., 1978). The paradigm of planning, program implementation, evaluation, feedback, and back to planning is a useful conception of evaluation's relationship to other elements of organizational functioning, but it must be recognized that other factors intrude as well. Cyert and March (1963) and Mintzberg (1973) have focused upon the effects of organizational goals, administrative structure, and communication networks, while Terreberry (1968) and Thompson (1967) have pointed to the influence of environment upon decision-making.

Investigations in the related field of research utilization have generated basic principles about the researcher-practitioner relationship which are applicable to the evaluator's functions as well. Thus, practitioners should participate in the evaluation's conception and performance; frequent and honest communications should occur between evaluators and practitioners to minimize obstructions and resistances; and there should be explicit delineations of evaluators' and practitioners' responsibilities for interpreting and communicating study findings (HIRI, 1976). Cox (1977) reanalyzed Mintzberg's (1973) studies of managerial work patterns and concluded that they have the following implications for human service program evaluators who seek to influence decision-making: (1) assessment data are but one of the information types considered by managers; (2) managers will utilize evaluation results only to the degree that they are perceived as relevant to the issues about which they are concerned; (3) managers are but casually concerned about the evaluation's methodological validity; and (4) evaluative data should be communicated verbally, succinctly, simply, and frequently.

When taken in their composite form, the issues and studies reviewed within Attkisson et al.'s (1978) framework could make even the most sophisticated of evaluators blanch at the task of pursuing organizational change based on assessment data. Nevertheless, the "cause" is just and evaluators must remain undeterred in the face of planned and unplanned obstacles. They must create equally formidable strategies for gaining the administrator's awareness and understanding of assessment data and willingness to give it the proper weight relative to other influences on the decision-making process. In the remainder of this overview we will highlight contributions of the authors of this monograph's papers to the analysis of how evaluators and managers may jointly pursue organizational effectiveness.

ENHANCING THE EVALUATOR'S EFFECTIVENESS

The familiar nature of organizational friction produced by the conflicting values and needs of researchers and clinicians leads Morell (Chapter 2) to critique prevailing notions of data relevance. He believes most research findings lack the power to solve highly intractable social problems; thus, he recommends an emphasis upon technological theory, which differs from scientific theory in the topics chosen for study and needed degrees of accuracy and precision. In contrast to laboratory-oriented researchers, technologically oriented evaluators are rewarded within the same problem-generating context and constraints surrounding decision-making program operators. Morell anticipates that within a technologically oriented framework evaluator-manager differences will pertain to technical and procedural issues, rather than to issues of fundamental philosophy and direction. He suggests that data utilization is enhanced when evaluators function as "development engineers" linking agency needs and social research capacities.

As procedures are refined for enhancing an evaluation's utility, analyses will be needed of whether this outcome actually is being achieved. Stevenson, Longabough, and McNeill (Chapter 3) present a metaevaluation model designed to clarify many of the confusions encountered in such determinations. They emphasize that evaluations serve diverse purposes and exercise their influence both within and outside the organization being studied. The criteria used in metaevaluations, therefore, must be selected relative to each assessment's particular purpose and intended impact. First, the findings' uses must be made explicit: for example, are they to affect a major policy decision or a procedural change, provide information feedback, generate new knowledge, or produce covert political action? Second, is the intended site of impact the organization being evaluated and/or similar agencies as well? For each of the grid cells produced by the two dimensions of decision relevance and locus of intended impact, Stevenson et al. suggest questions that can be used in assessing the extent to which an evaluator's utility expectations were met.

The need to explicate an evaluation's purpose is similarly emphasized by Carlson (Chapter 4) in his analysis of why management personnel often fail to grasp the evaluation's relevance to decision-making. Carlson asserts that the conceptual orientation of executives places greater emphasis upon responsiveness than clarity, and greater emphasis upon relationships than effectiveness. Evaluators concerned with utility, therefore, must be competent in expanding conceptual frameworks, aggregating alternative perspectives, and developing reliable data regarding key programmatic assumptions. Furthermore, rather than seeking to answer the question of which program direction is "best," evaluators should instead present the positive and negative implications of a more extended range of options. Carlson presents a model human services program and questions designed to clarify its political context, feasibility expectations, and outcome expectations. While the model's value in determining an evaluation's utility still is primarily heuristic, nevertheless, it does suggest various fresh perspectives from which to pursue empirical metaevaluations.

A markedly different strategy for enhancing evaluation's utility is presented by Windle (Chapter 5) in his review of why and how citizens should participate in the management of human service programs. Windle asserts that when professionals control a program's evaluation and determine the value structure within which the assessment is to be performed, citizen self-government is endangered. Examples of executives forced by public pressure to alter both direction and style are cited by Windle, and he contends that citizen participation in the evaluation process similarly would reduce administrative disregard for assessment-derived conclusions. A description of evaluations performed by citizens in various mental health settings is provided. Windle concludes that, despite obvious inadequacies, the growing frequency of "citizen studies" suggests their inherent face validity and feasibility.

Procedures for remedying obstacles to the utilization of evaluation findings concern Sproull and Larkey (Chapter 6). They identify the major obstacles as technical inadequacies in the evaluation's design and conduct which lead to flawed information and "delivery" inadequacies, such as providing administrators with data after the decision has been made. Focusing upon obstacles of the latter type, Sproull and Larkey propose solutions which could help the evaluator better understand managerial information-processing and decision-making. The extent to which prevailing modes of evaluator-manager interaction are likely to optimize utilization are considered, and the chapter expands upon Cox's (1977) previous work on managerial behavior pertinent to evaluation's utility.

The complexities of organizational functioning—particularly managerial behavior—are viewed by Broskowski, White, and Spector (Chapter 7) as significantly affecting evaluation's utility. An overview is presented of managerial operations and their purpose and practice are distinguished from evaluative operations. Executives, the authors note, often lack formal training for their positions and/or are deficient in both administrative and research theory. Value differences between executives and evaluators may complicate working relationships even further. Broskowski et al. emphasize the particular plight of middle managers who typically serve conflicting constituencies and urgently need evaluative information, but who have only a limited authority to utilize findings for program improvement. Examining evaluation from management's perspective, Broskowski et al. prescribe strategies for improving the evaluator's role effectiveness.

While the literature abounds with some cogent reasoning and much speculation about factors influencing evaluation's utility, empirically based analyses are less common. The final two chapters seek to fill this gap. While recognizably far from ideal in their design and analytic power, the studies by Weeks (Chapter 3) and Conner (Chapter 9) do illustrate potentialities and obstacles encountered in empirical metaevaluations of data's utility.

Employing a correlation design, Weeks explores the use of evaluative findings by a wide range of human service programs. The particular contribution of his investigation is its attempt to operationalize the following three variables frequently hypothesized as affecting utilization: (1) the evaluator's location in the organizational structure; (2) the methodological practices employed in generating and analyzing data; and (3) the context within which evaluative data can contribute to organizational decision-making. The correlations between utilization and variables 1 and 3 are found to be insignificant; the correlation with variable 2 is found significant at the .05 level. Weeks acknowledges limitations of the data, but he (rightly) asserts that far from perfect empirical metaevaluations are nevertheless an advance over armchair speculation. One refinement of Weeks' design would be to replace his unidimensional index of utilization with a more multifaceted measure of this dependent variable.

In the final chapter by Conner, six potential sources of evaluator-manager conflict are explored through a case study of a legal reform project's assessment. Conner places considerable, if not undue, emphasis upon the collegial relationship established between the evaluators and management as the factor responsible for minimal friction between these two groups and for the attention paid research findings. Again, limitations of the meta-evaluation's methodology are recognized by the author, particularly its failure to analyze plausible alternative explanations for the study's findings. However, a more rigorously designed case study could have great value in advancing our comprehension of whether and how evaluation findings contribute to organizational decision-making and practice.

REFERENCES

ATTKISSON, C. C. and W. A. HARGREAVES (1979) "A conceptual model for program evaluation in health organizations." Pp. 53-72 in H. C. Schulberg and F. Baker (eds.) Program Evaluation in the Health Fields (Vol. II). New York: Human Sciences Press.

ATTKISSON, C. C., T. R. BROWN, and W. A. HARGREAVES (1978) "Roles and functions of evaluation in human service programs." Pp. 59-96 in C. C. Attkisson, W. A. Hargreaves, M. Horowitz, and J. E. Sorenson (eds.) Evaluation of Human Service Programs. New York: Academic Press.

BEIGEL, A. (1974) "Evaluation on a shoestring." Pp. 16-31 in W. A. Hargreaves et al. (eds.) Resource Materials for Community Mental Health Program Evaluation. San Francisco: National Institute of Mental Health.

BIGELOW, D. (1975) "The impact of therapeutic effectiveness data on community mental health center management." Community Mental Health Journal 11:64-73.

BINNER, P. (1975) "Program evaluation." Pp. 342-383 in S. Feldman (ed.) The Administration of Mental Health Services. Springfield, IL: Charles C. Thomas.

CIARLO, J. (1974) Personal communication as cited by H. R. Davis and S. E. Salasin (1975) "The utilization of evaluation." Pp. 621-666 in E. L. Struening and M. Guttentag (eds.) Handbook of Evaluation Research. Beverly Hills, CA: Sage.

COHEN, L. H. (1977) "Factors affecting the utilization of mental health evaluation research findings." Professional Psychology 8:526-534.

COOK, T. and C. GRUDER (1978) "Meta-evaluation research." Evaluation Quarterly 2:5-51.

COX, G. B. (1977) "Managerial style: Implications for the utilization of program evaluation information." Evaluation Quarterly 1:499-509.

CYERT, R. M. and J. C. MARCH (1963) "A behavioral theory of the firm." Englewood Cliffs, NJ: Prentice-Hall.

EDWARDS, W., M. GUTTENTAG, and K. SNAPPER (1975) "A decision theoretic approach to evaluation research." Pp. 139-181 in E. L. Struening and M. Guttentag (eds.) Handbook of Evaluation Research. Beverly Hills, CA: Sage.

FELDMAN, S. (1975) "The administration of mental health services." Springfield, IL: Charles C Thomas.

FLANAGAN, J. C. (1976) "Case studies on the utilization of behavioral science research." In Human Interaction Research Institute, Putting Knowledge to Use. Los Angeles, CA: National Institute of Mental Health.

GLOCK, C. Y. (1976) "Applied social research: Some conditions affecting its utilization." In Human Interaction Research Institute, Putting Knowledge to Use. Los Angeles, CA: National Institute of Mental Health.

HIRI [Human Interaction Research Institute] (1976) Putting Knowledge to Use. Los Angeles, CA: National Institute of Mental Health.

HORST, P., J. N. NAY, J. W. SCANLON, and J. S. WHOLEY (1974) "Program management and the federal evaluator." Public Administration Review 34:300-308.

KRAUSE, M. (1978) "The interdependence of authority and evaluation." Presented at Third Annual Meeting of Evaluation Research Society, Washington, DC: November 2-4.

LYNN, L. E., JR. (1972) "Notes from HEW." Evaluation 1:24-28.

MINTZBERG, H. (1973) "The nature of managerial work." New York: Harper & Row.

NAGI, S. Z. (1976) "The practitioner as a partner in research." In Human Interaction Research Institute, Putting Knowledge to Use. Los Angeles, CA: National Institute of Mental Health.

PATTON, M. (1978) "Utilization-focused evaluation." Beverly Hills, CA: Sage.

ROSSI, P. H. (1971) "Evaluating social action programs." Pp. 276-280 in F. G. Caro (ed.) Readings in Evaluation Research. New York: Russell Sage Foundation.

ROSSMAN, B., D. HOBER and J. CIARLO (1979) "Awareness, use and consequences of evaluation data in a community mental health center." Community Mental Health Journal 15:7-16.

SCHULBERG, H., F. BAKER, and A. SHELDON (1969) "Program evaluation in the health fields." New York: Behavioral Publications.

TERREBERRY, S. (1968) "The evolution of organizational environments." Administrative Science Quarterly 12:590-613.

THOMPSON, J. D. (1967) "Organizations in action." New York: McGraw-Hill.

WEISS, C. H. (1972) "Evaluation research." Englewood Cliffs, NJ: Prentice-Hall.

WEISS, C. H. (1966) "Utilization of evaluation: Toward comparative study." Pp. 318-326 in C. H. Weiss (ed.) Evaluating Action Programs. Boston: Allyn & Bacon.

WHOLEY, J. S., J. W. SCANLON, H. G. DUFFY, J. S. FUKUMOTO, and L. M. VOGT (1970) "Federal evaluation policy: Analyzing the effects of public programs." Washington, DC: The Urban Institute.

WILDAVSKY, A. (1979) "The self-evaluating organization." Pp. 88-109 in H. C. Schulberg and F. Baker (eds.) Program Evaluation in the Health Fields (Vol. II). New York: Human Sciences Press.

WILDERMAN, R. (1979) "Evaluation research and the sociopolitical structure: A review." American Journal of Community Psychology 7:93-106.

WINDLE, C. and W. NEIGHER (1978) "Ethical problems in program evaluation: Advice for trapped evaluators." Evaluation and Program Planning 1:97-108.

Jonathan A. Morell
*The Hahnemann Medical College
and Hospital of Philadelphia*

2

EVALUATION AND SOCIAL SERVICE
An Analysis of Conflict
and Proposals for Change

This chapter has four objectives. First, it will explore roots of conflict between researchers and those who administer and plan social service programs. Second, it will argue that despite these problems, research must be carried out. In particular, there is a need for applied research in the form of outcome evaluation. Third, it will lay out a blueprint for evaluation as a technological rather than a scientific endeavor, and it will argue that evaluation information must be generalizable to a variety of settings. Finally, it will show that the technological model represents a set of organizing principles which will lead to the reduction of service agency-evaluator conflict and to the improvement of social programs.

EVALUATION-SERVICE AGENCY CONFLICT

Program evaluation is only a recent development in the continuing evolution of the social sciences (Flaherty and Morell,

AUTHOR'S NOTE: *This chapter was adapted from a paper presented at the second annual meeting of the Evaluation Research Society, L'enfant Plaza Hotel, Washington, D.C., November 2-4, 1978. The ideas presented here are developed more fully in a forthcoming book by the author:* Program Evaluation in Social Research.

21

1978). Therefore, it seems reasonable to analyze evaluation-service agency conflict in terms of the general problems of interface between social research and social science. Such an analysis yields several forces which bind the two worlds together.

Mutual need. Researchers need access to special populations, to particular types of information, and to social events that can be obtained only in social service settings. Further, a good deal of social theory has been developed within the social agency context. Once a research tradition is established, strong forces exist for continued work with and within that tradition (Kuhn, 1971). Social agencies, on the other hand, have their particular needs for social science. To some degree, at least, agencies seek to maximize service benefits, and such improvements ultimately cannot occur without the testing, research, and analysis provided by social scientists. Thus, social agencies serve as unique laboratories for social researchers and, in an indirect and convoluted way, agencies reap the benefits of that research.

Tradition. Two deep-seated beliefs bring research and social service together. First is the general belief in science's power and value. Although faith in science may have paled of late, it is certainly still one of our central beliefs. Second, there is the general belief that where problems exist, one should try to help. As a consequence of both beliefs, policy planners and administrators tend to seek the advice of social scientists. For their part, social scientists are willing to give advice, whether or not it is specifically sought.

Outside pressure. The notion that research can help solve social problems is held not only by researchers and those planning social services, but also by the general public and those who set policy and control resources. This produces an additional force for cooperation between research and agency—the power of the purse.

TYPES OF RESEARCH-AGENCY FRICTIONS

Social science theories are often perceived by nonresearchers as having little value for explaining the cause of social problems or, presumably, pointing the way to the problems' solutions (Bloom, 1972). Consequently, research based on those theories will spark the same types of disagreements. Further, issues of considerable concern to planners or administrators may be of little interest to social scientists.

A second type of conflict stems from the dislocation that research or evaluation can cause to the everyday workings of an agency. Insuring smooth standard operating practices is undoubtedly one of the administrator's chief concerns. The intrusion of research and data collection procedures certainly allows ample opportunity for interfering with established routines.

Third, disagreements are likely to occur concerning who should control the research. Administrators are ultimately responsible for everything occurring within their organization; thus, it is legitimate that they have a say in agency research. However, researchers have a similar responsibility to their work. What is to happen when agency and research needs do not coincide?

Fourth, evaluation apprehension is always a problem. Evaluation is often implied in any act of observation and research. The apprehension is worse when the research is explicitly evaluative. Etzioni (1969) argues that although organizations can legitimately invest resources in both maintenance objectives and stated service goals, many evaluators implicitly assume that all resources are being invested in the goals of service. Campbell (forthcoming) emphasizes that advocacy is bound to involve exaggerated or inflated claims. If this is true, and if one considers organizational members as advocates for the organization's goals and objectives, it is easy to appreciate evaluation apprehension. Rossi (1972) argues that the impact of social programs will, of necessity, be small, since only the more difficult problems remain for us to solve and they defy solution. Weiss (1972) argues that although social problems must be dealt with by multiple-cause models, funding structures allow only single-cause solutions. If there is any truth to these arguments, it is a small wonder that service agency personnel fear the researcher's scrutiny when even a hint of evaluation is present.

Finally, a "culture gap" exists between researchers and service agency personnel. Researchers tend to seek generality and similarity between discrete events or people. Practitioners, in contrast, tend to emphasize the unique attributes of each client (Bloom, 1972). Researchers like to deal with the development of knowledge that may have long-range beneficial effects; practitioners are usually preoccupied with immediate patient needs (Bergen, 1969). Inherent in the notion of research is development and change. Inherent in administration are efforts at maintaining an organization's steady state (Caro, 1971). A researcher's status is bound up with the *process* of finding out, while the status of practitioners is bound to helping individuals by the application of a specific body of knowledge. Administrators gain status by maintaining a smoothly operating organization. Researchers gain status by publishing research (Bergen, 1969). The cultural gap also includes different perspectives on the ethics of control groups, randomization, and other accouterments of experimental design (Mann, 1971; Riecken and Boruch, 1974). Finally, researchers and administrators organize and conceptualize their work differently. Researchers are immediately interested in the causal relationships among dependent and independent variables. These relationships should also be of great importance to administrators, since such knowledge would help them determine organizational effectiveness. However, attainment of program goals is probably not the real, practical, everyday concern of administrators who are preoccupied with insuring the smooth interplay of organizational units such as personnel, services, and departments. The interplay between such units may, of course, be related ultimately to program goals, but what percentage of anyone's day is devoted to "ultimates"? Thus, the immediate concern of researchers is the distant concern of administrators who do not wish to confront long-range goals while enmeshed in the daily battle for survival.

On balance, it may seem best for research merely to "go away" and permit hard-pressed service personnel to function as best they can under difficult circumstances. In fact, there is much justification for the widespread implementation of research and evaluation.

THE CASE FOR RESEARCH AND EVALUATION

The best argument for conducting research in social service settings is that the knowledge gained has value in its own right. We should not be a society that measures everything by the metric of practical utility.

Over and above the aesthetics of knowledge, other powerful considerations dictate the necessity of research and evaluation. First, the practical value of much research is not always immediately apparent. If the justification for investigation is tied too closely to practical concerns, much important and potentially useful work is likely to be left undone. Second, social programs are not isolated, to be protected at all costs from negative criticism. Given the public nature of the social service enterprise, there is an obligation to assess how well a solution is working, and to engage in activities which may lead to better solutions.

The "public obligation" argument contains yet another aspect: most attempts at solving social problems are planned with the full knowledge that the programs to be initiated are inadequate. Some attempt at solving problems is better than no attempt, and serious problems demand attention. On the other hand, that rationale implies that inefficient solutions will be institutionalized and perpetuated. The institutionalization of poor solutions cannot be tolerated, and when efforts are known to be inadequate there is an obligation to use already institutionalized programs as opportunities for finding better solutions.

These reasons lead to the conclusion that social programs cannot shut out the activities of researchers and evaluators, but persuasive logic alone will not overcome the real and legitimate problems arising from the "forced marriage" of social service and social research. That relationship must be organized in such a manner that the needs of all parties will be served. The new structure must take cognizance of existing problems and contain a set of organizing principles which will allow mutually agreeable solutions to those problems. The remainder of this chapter outlines such a plan.

MAKING EVALUATION RELEVANT

While pure research is legitimate, the bulk of research in service agency settings must be aimed at solving practical problems. What should the nature of "practical research" be? I believe that it must take the form of generalizable outcome evaluation that is oriented toward the long-range improvement of social programs. Further, this research should be based on a technological model of research.

The Need for Generalizability

The process of information utilization for practical decision-making has a dynamic all its own. The process is slow, convoluted, and diffuse. Although it can be speeded up, it will always remain a formidable difficulty. Further, attempts at immediate relevancy are likely to produce evaluation results which are not generalizable. Given the slow pace of the utilization process, and given the tradeoff between generalizability and immediacy, attempts at immediate utility of evaluation are bound to produce results which are of little value for any purpose.

A second reason for long-range perspectives stems from the need to replicate research. Any study, no matter how well designed, may yield idiosyncratic results. Thus, unless evaluation findings are replicated, a reliable knowledge base about the effectiveness of social programs cannot be built up. Such a knowledge base is crucial to the discovery of substantive new solutions to problems.

Finally, Brandl (1978) has argued that political decision-making is not based on the outcome of programs. Rather, politicians judge the value of a program by the number of constituencies that had a say in its establishment. Success is defined as making decisions based on as wide a consensus as possible, not on the outcome of those decisions. If there is any truth to this argument, evaluators must aim their information at the constituencies that influence decision makers. This will take a considerably longer time than it would to influence a relatively few key decision makers.

In sum, quick-draw contests on evaluation utility will have the long-range effect of building a body of information which is not relevant to ever-changing needs and which was not utilized at the time when it was relevant.

Evaluation as Technology

If evaluation is reconceptualized as a technological enterprise, it will be possible to ameliorate many of the problems of relevance which have plagued social research.

Critiques of relevance. Gergen (1973) claims that although the techniques of social research may be scientific and objective, the content of scientific theories is not. Rather, the content of theories is based on "acquired dispositions" which come from the culture in which researchers are embedded. Contemporary culture is always changing in many ways, and it is not surprising that social scientific theories do not remain consonant with that change. Similarly, it might be argued that the theoretical base and orientations of evaluators are not easily brought into consonance with the needs of their audiences and that, as a result, the relevance of evaluation information leaves much to be desired.

The "culture gap" between social researchers and social agency administrators has already been discussed. The lack of understanding generated by this gap may well be another reason why evaluators do not seem responsive to the needs of administrators and policy makers.

The basic goal of science is to discover what is true, and this pursuit often involves the use of methodologies which may not be applicable to complex social phenomena. Argyris (1975), for example, claims that experiments require a high degree of control over subjects and the advocacy of a very limited and well-defined course of action. Further, Argyris claims that because of these constraints, the results of experiments may not be applicable to complex nonexperimental situations.

An essential element of discovering truth and building theory is the development of "simplistic models" which approximately reflect the phenomenon being studied (Kaplan, 1964: ch. 7). It may be, however, that these models are too delicate and simplistic to allow the prediction of events in complex, uncontrolled settings. Thus, the models which are so useful in allowing the study of subtle relationships may be inadequate—and thus irrelevant—in the complex world of social programming.

Another critique of relevance deals with the choice of topics for study. Political or theoretical influences may steer people's attention away from topics which would be of importance for practical decision making.

Finally, there is Rossi's (1972) argument that research is simply too weak to help solve intractable social problems. If there is any validity to this analysis, it is easy to see why the finding of researchers and evaluators are considered irrelevant. Technological models of research provide a framework for evaluation which reduces many of the blocks to relevance cited above.

The technological solution. The essence of technological research is an attempt to find solutions which make a practical difference in the world of everyday problem-solving. Good technological theory is theory that provides a useful guide to those solutions. It does not necessarily have to be true. In contrast, the essence of scientific thinking involves the discovery of truth and the building of theory. There is no logical requirement for such truth-seeking to have practical implications.

Science and technology also differ in the manner in which topics are chosen for study. Scientists are duty-bound to carefully invest their efforts in answering questions which will clear up conceptual difficulties, determine the truth of a speculation, or advance the development of theory. There is no requirement that the questions must have practical value. Technologists, on the other hand, seek questions which further the control of factors which are immediate, powerful in the practical world, and manipulable within the constraints of specific practical contexts (Jarvie, 1972; Skolimowski, 1972).

Finally, technology and science differ in their needs for accuracy and precision. Since small deviations from a prediction may have major theoretical implications, scientists invest considerable resources in making all measurements as accurate as possible within the bounds of practicality and appropriate levels of measurement. Such efforts, however, direct resources away from other considerations and also may provide more detailed information than is needed for a particular practical decision. Technologists, on the other hand, must choose levels of accuracy specifically with practical applications in mind; hence they must consider the needs of decision makers in the planning of their research.

In sum, technologists are rewarded for efficiently operating within the same problem-generating context and sets of constraints which surround practical decision makers. Theory is judged by its practical utility. Questions for study are aimed at issues which make a difference in the real world. Levels of accuracy are adjusted for the needs of decision makers and their freedom to operate. Although both scientists and technologists may be interested in solving practical problems, there is no *logical* connection between priorities for scientific study and the importance of practical problems. There is such a connection when technological models are followed. Thus, technological perspectives bring the "cultures" of researchers and administrators together, and such a merger allows many steps to be taken which will further increase cooperation between the parties.

STEPS TO INCREASE
EVALUATION-AGENCY COOPERATION

Two types of changes are needed. First, problems must be identified which can be lessened by increased mutual understanding. Second, plans must be laid which will lead to substantive changes in how evaluation is carried out.

In terms of mutual understanding, several areas are crucial. Evaluators must appreciate the disruption they can cause by requesting changes in agency procedures, and by imposing research/analytic perspectives on already-developed professional philosophies. Second, evaluators and researchers must take the concept of "relevance" seriously—overused words lose their meaning, and people who overuse words lose their credibility. Finally, researchers and evaluators must try to gain an honest appreciation of the types of problems that service providers, administrators, and policy makers really need solved.

For their part, agency personnel also have lessons to learn. First, almost no research or evaluation will have immediate applicability, and some perspective on this matter must be gained. Second, agency personnel must realize that some very important issues cannot be studied without the help of service-providing contexts. Finally, agency personnel must realize that almost no research can be completely unobtrusive: once the legitimacy of a particular study is recognized, the inevitability of some inconvenience must be accepted.

All parties to research and evaluation must learn to appreciate the limits of research and of scientific methods. Unfortunately, all of these efforts at understanding—even if fully achieved— would not solve all problems. Mutual understanding does not resolve substantive conflict, it only clarifies the nature of that conflict. Difficulties can, however, be lessened and substantive efforts can be taken to achieve that end. Recognition can be given to personnel who supply data, either by keeping people abreast of the progress of research, by paying people for their time, or simply by adopting the attitude that those who supply data are experts without whose time and effort a project could not be carried out.

Researchers and evaluators can be taught management skills along with the courses in research, statistics, and specialized content areas. The aim would not be to turn researchers into managers; it would, however, sensitize evaluators to problems which may arise and alert people to possible solutions to those problems. Similarly, administrators, policy makers, and service delivery personnel can be taught research and evaluation. Such programs can carry academic credit or other similar recognition for achievement, and would serve several purposes. First, they may help people gain professional credibility, knowledge, and increased job mobility potential. Second, such programs would give people a sense of how to constructively work with those who have expertise in research and evaluation. Finally, it would sensitize nonresearchers to the difficulties and problems of carrying out adequate research or evaluation work.

Agency cooperation in evaluation or research might be traded for specialized information. Presumably, evaluators have the ability to generate information which is of great importance to an agency, but which may not be available in the normal course of events. In such cases it might be legitimate to divert some research or evaluation efforts for the purpose of collecting that information, even if the effort would siphon resources from the main intent of the research or evaluation.

The evaluation profession might do well to further develop the concept of the "development engineer" (Cherns, 1971). This would be a professional whose job is to explore links between developments in social research and the needs of service agencies. There is ample precedent for this type of work, as evidenced by the literature on "linking agents" and "organizational change agents" (Bennis et al., 1976: Chin, 1976). Perhaps such a role should be formalized or expanded. In any case, researchers and evaluators should make efforts to play such a role whenever possible.

Another solution might be for evaluators to make more use of multiple measures of success. The "distance" between a treatment and an effect can exist on many levels. By measuring several of those levels, it becomes possible to maintain scientific integrity, while at the same time helping programs show that they have had some good results. As an example, consider the evaluation of a marriage counseling program which included measures of the following factors: Do couples believe that the counseling helped them? Do couples argue less at various intervals after counseling? During the year after treatment, has the counseling reduced the divorce rate? The first measure is almost certain to put the program in a positive light. The other measures are progressively less likely to show positive results. But each is a legitimate measure of impact, and each contains information which may help improve the counseling program.

Finally, it may be worthwhile to consider establishing a formal mechanism to mediate conflict, to explore general and specific solutions, to educate all parties involved, and to disseminate information which may be useful in resolving conflict.

Even under the best of circumstances, the suggestions given above cannot eliminate all difficulties. Researcher-agency frictions involve a complex interplay of forces which make many problems intractable. Although any given solution may help, attempts are likely to be very weak in relation to the complexity and difficulty of the problem involved. These solutions would have a much better chance of success through a basic shift of perspective in which a truly common meeting ground is established for all the parties involved. Such a change is embodied in the conceptualization of evaluation as a technological endeavor.

CONFLICT RESOLUTION
IN A TECHNOLOGICAL PERSPECTIVE

Individual steps to conflict resolution stand a chance of having noticeable impact when evaluation is cast in a technological mold. Communication and understanding begin to have an effect because both parties work within the same context of generating questions, determining constraints, and prioritizing needs. There still will be differences between the parties, but the difference will involve technical and procedural issues, rather than basic issues of philosophy and direction.

Applications experts with a technological knowledge base are more likely to find innovations which may appeal to decision makers and thus will not have to strain imagination and credibility when trying to "sell" the virtues of research and evaluation.

Multiple measures of success become more useful because of agreed-upon beliefs of what variables are important, which are most powerful, and which are most likely to make a difference in the real world. Mediators and ombudsmen will no longer have to reconcile fundamentally opposed views; hence, their efforts are likely to achieve actual success.

In sum, the technological perspective imposes the same frame of reference on researchers and evaluators which normally operates in the world of practical decision-making. That is the great contribution of the technological perspective. Once it is adopted, all sources of friction become less intractable and, as a result, any single solution has some chance for success. Evaluation results still will not be immediately applicable, as the need for generalizability will remain, and evaluators still will have different needs than administrators. However, the accruing knowledge base will begin to be truly relevant, and social service will begin to look to the knowledge and expertise of evaluators as a source of helping to improve society's solutions to social problems.

CONCLUSION

A historical analysis of the interface between social research and social service makes it clear that the present difficulties are long standing and largely intractable. Despite these problems, service agencies have an obligation to work at improving their programs, and that improvement depends largely on the knowledge-generating potential of the research perspective. Evaluation must attempt to generate information that will be generalizable to the continually shifting needs and priorities of society. Because of the slow pace of information utilization, attempts at immediate utility of evaluation will generate information that will be neither valid nor relevant by the time it is attended to.

Evaluation must be organized around technological principles. Technological models will give evaluators and decision makers a common frame of reference for determining needs, priorities, and acceptable solutions. Once such a frame of reference is adapted, there is a realistic chance that specific attempts at decreasing evaluation-service friction will succeed.

Friction-reducing attempts must proceed on two levels. First, efforts must be increased to promote mutual understanding. Second (and more important), substantive changes must be made in the way evaluation work is organized.

The evaluation and service communities have legitimate differences, and it is not likely that problems will be wholly resolved. However, if specific solutions are attempted within a conducive frame of reference, both groups will benefit.

REFERENCES

ARGYRIS, C. (1975) "Dangers in applying results from experimental social psychology." American Psychologist 30: 469-485.
BENNIS, W. G., K. D. BENNE, R. CHIN, and K. E. COREY [eds.] (1976) The Planning of Change. New York: Holt, Rinehart & Winston.
BERGEN, B. J. (1969) "Professional communities and the evaluation of demonstration projects in community mental health." Pp. 121-135 in H. C. Schulberg, A. Sheldon, and F. Baker (eds.) Program Evaluation in the Health Fields. New York: Behavioral Publications.
BLOOM, B. C. (1972) "Mental health program evaluation." In S. E. Golann and C. Eisdorfer (eds.) Handbook of Community Mental Health. New York: Appleton-Century-Crofts.
BRANDL, J. E. (1978) "Evaluation and politics." Evaluation (Special Issue): 6-7.
CAMPBELL, D. T. (forthcoming) "Methods for the experimenting society." American Psychologist.
CARO, F. G. (1971) "Evaluation research—An overview." In F. G. Caro (ed.) Readings in Evaluation Research. New York: Russell Sage Foundation.
CHERNS, A. (1971) "Social research and its diffusion." In F. G. Caro (ed.) Readings in Evaluation Research. New York: Russell Sage Foundation.
CHIN, R. (1976) "The utility of system models and development models for practitioners." Pp. 90-102 in W. G. Bennis, K. D. Benne, R. Chin, and K. E. Corey (eds.) The Planning of Change. New York: Holt, Rinehart & Winston.
ETZIONI, A. (1969) "Two approaches to organizational analysis: A critique and a suggestion." In H. C. Schulberg, A. Sheldon, and F. Baker (eds.) Program Evaluation in the Health Fields. New York: Behavioral Publications.
FLAHERTY, E. W. and J. A. MORELL (1978) "Evaluation: Manifestations of a new field." Evaluation and Program Planning 1: 1-9.
GERGEN, K. J. (1973) "Social psychology as history." Journal of Personality and Social Psychology 26: 309-320.

JARVIE, I. C. (1972) "Technology and the structure of knowledge." Pp. 54-61 in C. Mitcham and R. Mackey (eds.) Philosophy and Technology. New York: Free Press.

KAPLAN, A. (1964) The Conduct of Inquiry: Methodology for Behavioral Sciences. Scranton, PA: Chandler.

KUHN, T. S. (1971) The Structure of Scientific Revolutions. Chicago: University of Chicago Press.

MANN, J. (1971) "Technical and social difficulties in the conduct of evaluative research." In F.G. Caro (ed.) Readings in Evaluation Research. New York: Russell Sage Foundation.

RIECKEN, H. and R. F. BORUCH [eds.] (1974) Social Experimentation: A Method for Planning and Evaluating Social Interventions. New York: Academic Press.

ROSSI, P. H. (1972) "Boobytraps and pitfalls in the evaluation of social action programs." Pp. 224-235 in C. Weiss (ed.) Evaluating Action Programs: Readings in Social Action Research. Boston: Allyn & Bacon.

SKOLIMOWSKI, H. (1972) "The structure of thinking in technology." In C. Mitcham & R. Mackey (eds.), Philosophy and Technology. New York: Free Press.

WEISS, C. (1972) "The politicization of evaluation research." In C. Weiss (ed.) Evaluating Action Programs: Readings in Social Action Research. Boston: Allyn & Bacon.

John F. Stevenson
University of Rhode Island

Richard H. Longabaugh
Butler Hospital and Brown University

Dwight N. McNeill
Butler Hospital

3

METAEVALUATION
IN THE HUMAN SERVICES

Evaluators frequently bemoan their lack of impact on decisions made by the clients they serve (Weiss, 1973; Davis and Salasin, 1975; Brown et al., 1978). Mental health and other human service evaluators are among those who are deeply concerned about this issue (Mechanic, 1975; Windle, 1976), but, unlike the case in other areas of evaluation, the concern has not yet led to the development of models for examining the merit of evaluation studies. We believe that this kind of examination, increasingly called "metaevaluation" (Scriven, 1969; Stufflebeam, 1974, 1978; Cook and Gruder, 1978), can be fruitfully applied to aid human services evaluators in effectively influencing decision makers.

Our approach to the development of a metaevaluation model suitable for application in human service organizations begins with a review of pertinent literature, proceeds to a discussion of

AUTHOR'S NOTE: *This chapter is a condensed version of a paper delivered at the 1978 Annual Meeting of the Evaluation Research Society in Washington, DC. For a complete version, including an appendix containing the questionnaire developed by the authors, please contact the first author.*

a number of problems encountered in developing the model, and closes with a presentation of the model itself. We will argue that (1) the typical role of evaluators in human service settings creates special concerns for these evaluators about their impact on management, (2) a specialized form of purpose-oriented metaevaluation can guide improved responses by these evaluators to their perceived ineffectiveness, and (3) technical adequacy of evaluation efforts is a necessary but not sufficient means toward the ultimate end of policy impact.

MODELS FOR METAEVALUATION

A number of authorities on evaluation have presented explanations for inadequate impact of evaluation studies on managerial decisions. These suggested reasons for low evaluation impact have one element in common: they imply a need for systematic evaluation of evaluation activities themselves. Scriven (1969) coined the term "metaevaluation" for this process; this chapter will use that term to refer to various attempts to make judgments on the merit of evaluation work. There are as many potential conceptions of metaevaluation as there are of evaluation itself. Cook and Gruder (1978:6), for example, use "the term 'meta-evaluation' to refer only to the evaluation of summative evaluation—studies where the data are collected directly from program participants within a systematic design framework." Citing a number of reasons for poor technical quality in current summative evaluations, they go on to propose a classification scheme for models of metaevaluation, all of which focus on assessing methodological rigor. Stufflebeam's (1974) model adds utility and cost to technical adequacy as criteria for good evaluation. Specific components of utility which Stufflebeam (1974) has described include relevance, scope, importance, credibility, timeliness, and pervasiveness of dissemination. The present proposal owes a great deal to Stufflebeam's work.

The literature on effective dissemination of findings to insure their utilization can also be considered metaevaluative in its orientation (Schulberg and Baker, 1969; HIRI, 1970). Fair-weather et al. (1974) studied a nationwide dissemination effort in mental health using adoption as the criterion to test the value of a number of dissemination strategy alternatives and organizational characteristics. Davis and Salasin (1975) have proposed a comprehensive model to enhance the impact of evaluation. Murrell (1976) has indicated a number of "conversion techniques" to improve utilization of evaluation. Cohen (1977) has summarized many prior findings on the variables which affect utilization of mental health evaluation research findings. These authors provide some parameters and a set of guidelines for planning, executing, and reporting evaluations with decision impact as the ultimate criterion for success.

Despite contrasts between those who seek rigor and those who seek immediate utility, a literature is gradually accumulating on a variety of metaevaluative responses to evaluators' concern about their lack of impact. Davis and Salasin (1975:626) come closest to our view when they suggest that "better tracer evaluations of evaluation utilization itself would offer more reinforcement to evaluators." They advocate the evaluation of evaluation by those who work on a continuing basis within human service organizations, and point out that little has been done in this area.

THE ROLE OF THE EVALUATOR
IN THE HUMAN SERVICES

The role of evaluators working within political contexts will affect the criteria they select for evaluating the merit of their own work. Few commentators on evaluation in the human services make a plea for classical experimental rigor, and the dominant view appears to be that administrators should be given what they can use while they can still use it (Hargreaves et al., 1977). The typical role of human service evaluators as employees in the organization under scrutiny provides a strong incentive to be relevant for managerial decisions. As insiders, human service evaluators are subject to different kinds of political pressures and different sources of information (Bennett and Lumsdaine, 1975; Cohen, 1977). Another hallmark of human service evaluators is the multiplicity of clients and targets with which they may deal simultaneously and the multiple, sometimes conflicting roles they may play as quality assurers, summative program evaluators, formative peer-evaluators, and information monitors (Lundy, 1978; Murrell and Brown, 1977). The development of a meta-evaluation model for application to the human services will require attention to the special nature of the evaluation enter-prise encountered there in order to identify the particular pur-poses made likely by the typical roles of evaluators in these settings.

PURPOSES FOR EVALUATION

When evaluators in human services organizations bother to stop whatever they're doing and ask themselves, "Why am I doing this evaluation?," they may come up with some answers which are not very closely related to the classifications of evaluation pur-poses commonly found in the literature on evaluation. The answers may be even more divergent when, several months after an evaluation report has been circulated, evaluators ask them-selves, "What was my evaluation really used for?" Obtaining answers to these questions delineates the focus of criteria for successful evaluation.

The literature offers important, though not entirely satisfying, classification schemes for evaluation purposes. In most dis-cussions, purposes are grouped into two, three, or four major types. One such type reflects a purpose toward which virtually all human services evaluators direct some effort—accountability to external requirements. Stufflebeam (1974), Murrell and Brown (1977), McIntyre et al. (1977), and Coursey (1977) (among others) have included this as a central purpose, although they do not share a precise definition. In general, the term is used to refer to required data-collection and data-reporting activities which allow comparison of the target for evaluation to some externally imposed criterion for performance or cost-effectiveness. The primary client is an external body which can impose sanctions to compel conformity with its demands. A major problem with the term accountability is that it indicates a type of client rather than a type of purpose, since the use to which the client intends to put the evaluation can range from none (except to meet the rules by which the client must operate), to program improvement, to program termination. Most common is a routine monitoring function to compel minimally acceptable adherence to standards for service delivery.

The term "accountability" is less likely to be applied when a powerful *internal* client (such as an administrative director) requires evaluation of an organizational component against some criteria (implicit or explicit) or a comparison group. In these cases the evaluation is likely to be referred to as "formative" or "summative" (Scriven, 1967). It probably would be termed summative, or retroactive (Stufflebeam, 1974), if there is a reasonable possibility that the decision-making client will view the evaluation as an ultimate judgment on the worth of the target of the evaluation, with the potential for a decision to discontinue, expand, export, or greatly modify the target. As was noted in the discussion of accountability, the client for a summative judgment also can be external to the organization in which the evaluator works.

When, on the other hand, the client desires to develop a new program on the basis of a pilot operation, or to continually modify and improve an ongoing program, the terms "formative," "pro-active," and "developmental" are likely to be applied to describe the nature of the evaluation (Scriven, 1967; Stufflebeam, 1974; Murrell and Brown, 1977). Note that the terms "formative" and "summative" become more ambiguous when they are applied to evaluations of ongoing operations which are embedded in the organizational structure of the institution. A distinction has been made here between evaluations whose impacts may include program termination and evaluations whose intended purposes extend only as far as program improvements, but this distinction is not precisely equivalent to various presentations of "formative" and "summative" in the literature. In a hierarchically structured organization an internal evaluation may be done with clients at several levels of the hierarchy (for example, a top-level administrator as well as the chief administrator of a program targeted for evaluation) which may make the evaluation simultaneously formative and summative.

Despite some confusion regarding the precise application of the terms described above, they all share one common thread which is clearly appropriate for an examination of the evaluator as part of a feedback loop—all refer to kinds of evaluation useful for furthering what Bennett and Lumsdaine (1975) have called "service goals": that is, they refer to evaluation whose goal is to be used in decision-making in the short run, to be relevant for specific clients' needs. In contrast with this group of purposes, Bennett and Lumsdaine set up a second broad category of "understanding-relevant" evaluation, whose purpose is to further "research goals." Similar distinctions have been made by Coursey (1977), who refers to "theory building" purposes, and by Murrell and Brown (1977) in their discussion of "demonstration." Admittedly, these distinctions are not entirely clear. The contrast appears to rest on the role of immediate information needs in determining the planning and implementation of the evaluation, and this in turn is usually linked to the presence of a primary client empowered and intending to make significant short-run decisions.

As this brief summary of the literature shows, terms for classifying evaluation purposes are abundant, but they provide an ambiguous system for categorizing human service evaluations.

PROBLEMS IN CLASSIFYING PURPOSES

In order to gain a clearer view of the range of purposes for evaluation and a measure of success in achieving them, we have attempted to design a questionnaire which would quantify both the evaluator's and the client's perceptions of intentions and results. The exercise may have produced more questions than answers. Before describing a tentative resolution of the difficulties raised by the effort at quantification, we will present some problems foreshadowed in the literature review. Since the authors' experience is in evaluation in an inpatient psychiatric setting, the examples will be drawn from this setting.

The multiple-client problem. The term "client" is used here to refer to persons who request an evaluation, who will use the report, and who have the power to take meaningful action based on the report. Clients often are those who control the financial resources with which the evaluation is done. In the case of a typical program evaluation study in our institution, a medical director initially may request an evaluation of a target program, and the program director may participate actively in planning and conducting the evaluation. These two clients may have very different ideas about the purposes for which the evaluation should be used. Evaluators have their own analysis of the politics of the situation and hopes for the impact of the evaluation which may not coincide with those of other clients. Who is the primary client? Clarifying the identity of the clients for the evaluation is important because so much evaluation is directed at specific client needs. In order to answer a question about purposes one must know *whose* purposes. Ths is apparent as soon as one gets beneath the rhetoric of shared ultimate aims (for example, "improving mental health in the community") to specific objectives, decisions, and indices. How can the success of an evaluation be judged when multiple and conflicting purposes coexist?

Overt versus covert purposes. The formally stated purposes for an evaluation activity may be supplemented or overwhelmed by any number of unstated intentions for its use. These covert intentions may be held by any or all evaluation clients. Administrators, for example, may wish to postpone making a difficult decision or may wish to accumulate some "hard data" to support a decision they have already made but not yet announced. Evaluators may have their own covert purposes for evaluation, such as the quest for greater power and influence. Covert purposes are generally political, in the sense that they deal with the acquisition, maintenance, and redistribution of power in the organization. Although openly taking account of such purposes in planning and reporting an evaluation may be foolhardy, it would be equally foolish to leave them out of intended outcomes for evaluation activities, since they are sometimes central aspects of impact.

Means versus ends. As has been indicated, the literature on metaevaluation (Stufflebeam, 1974; Cook and Gruder, 1978) has focused largely on the methodological soundness of an evaluation study as the criterion for its worth. Other proposed criteria have dealt with timeliness, relevance, understandability, and absence of bias (Stufflebeam, 1974; Murrell and Brown, 1977). Cohen (1977) has gone further by suggesting such possible goals as (1) awareness of results by administrators, (2) consideration of results during decision-making, (3) a resultant policy consistent with evaluation findings, and (4) diffusion to other settings. Cohen selects the second of his goals as most reasonable. One could go beyond his list altogether and suggest improved attainment of organizational objectives as the ultimate criterion. This list of possible criteria spans a continuum very similar to the process-outcome dimension which evaluators use in thinking about the target for their evaluations. In judging evaluation success one might set as the objective a satisfactorily implemented evaluation process, a clear and unambiguous report at the termination of the project, and/or tangible results in organizational behavior. As in the case of evaluation of service programs, the present authors find it essential to define ultimate purposes in terms of outcomes—that is, in terms of impacts on the organization or the wider world which are clearly linked to evaluation activities. Criteria such as appropriate methodology, timeliness, and lack of bias are viewed as means to these ends, and in many cases as logical prerequisites. However, it is much easier to assess success in achieving the means than the ends. This makes it tempting to assume that a valid, readable, timely, and pertinent evaluation report naturally will have the intended effect, or at least that one reasonably cannot be held to the attainment of purposes beyond these. But we all have larger objectives in mind, and in the long run we are held accountable to them.

The problems raised above may help to explain the absence of an empirical literature on metaevaluation in the human services. The models provided by metaevaluators have not lent themselves readily to the needs of human service evaluators due to the special role demands experienced by such evaluators. In addition, the confusing multiplicity of clients, the concern for impact as well as proper execution, and the function of covert purposes for evaluation make it difficult to quantify dimensions of evaluation merit. In the next section a classification scheme for evaluation purposes will be proposed which attempts to confront these difficulties. It should be noted that this system is not intended to imply mutual exclusivity of multiple purposes. Indeed, the several simultaneous roles that the evaluator is often expected to play guarantee diversity and complexity of purpose.

A PROPOSAL FOR
CLASSIFYING INTENDED PURPOSES

Our model for purposive evaluation is based on the view that evaluators can improve their utility by examining their purposes carefully during the planning phase of an evaluation activity and by retrospectively evaluating their success in achieving their purposes. We propose that the desired impact of human service evaluation can be located along two dimensions (see Figure 1). One of these concerns the extent of planned decision relevance, and the other concerns the intended locus of impact. As has been emphasized, evaluators hired on a full-time, continuing basis within an organization are likely to be primarily oriented toward local and immediate impact. Secondarily, they may be concerned with long-term local usefulness of their work. Usually lowest in priority is external application.

Decision relevance and locus of intended impact can be used to create a grid within which the variety of purposes for evaluation can be classified. For each cell a series of questions can be asked

| | Site of Intended Impact | |
Decision Relevance	Evaluation Site	Generalized
Major Decision	Explicit potential for major program change	Planned dissemination of an innovative program, if effective
Recommendations for Procedural Changes	Anticipated changes in procedures and practices	Planned dissemination of technical innovations
Information Feedback	Monitoring of meaningful performance indices	Exportable norms for performance
Knowledge	Establishment of local cause-effect sequences	Establishment of generalizable cause-effect sequences; improvement in evaluation methodology
Covert Political Impact	Shifts in relative power, or maintenance of power	

Figure 1: Purposes for Evaluation in the Human Services

to determine the extent to which evaluators and clients intended a study to fulfill particular purposes, and the extent to which their expectations were met. In each cell the criteria for appropriate design, execution, reporting, and impact are somewhat different, and the relevant range of the means-ends continuum can be reflected in the questions asked. In the paragraphs that follow each cell is briefly described.

Sometimes evaluations are intended to be used to make major decisions within the organization in which the evaluation is done, and these decisions are fairly explicit prior to the study. Examples of this are (1) a program which will be terminated, expanded, or completely overhauled as a result of the study; and (2) review of a central policy of the organization, with an explicit alternative policy in mind (this would include needs assessments if they could produce significant changes in organizational objectives). Criteria for success would include (1) relevance of the measures used for the intended decisions; (2) plausibility of the results in terms of design rigor; (3) timeliness of the report; (4) clarity of the report, especially of its conclusions; (5) circulation to the relevant clients; (6) role of the evaluation, relative to other factors, in affecting targeted decisions; and (7) magnitude of decision impact on the organization.

Sometimes evaluations are intended to culminate in a series of recommendations by the evaluator for specific changes in procedures, even though no major decision has been specified in advance. Examples of this are (1) evaluation of the quality of services provided for a particular kind of clientele and (2) evaluation of a service program to improve it. Criteria for success would include (1) reliability and absence of bias as a description of reality; (2) explicitness of recommendations; (3) clear connection between recommendations and data; (4) circulation to the relevant clients; (5) proportion of recommendations adopted; and (6) measurable changes in organizational functioning in the intended direction.

Sometimes an evaluation is intended to provide feedback about various aspects of organizational functioning which can be compared by clients with established criteria or previous performance. In such cases the evaluators generally do not expect to make specific recommendations. An example of this is quarterly reporting of clients served, services delivered, and other such information. Criteria for success would include (1) reliability and absence of bias in the measures; (2) validity of measures as indications of pertinent aspects of organizational functioning; (3) clarity of the report; (4) assimilation of the report by clients; and (5) responsive actions by clients if they are implicated by the findings.

Sometimes evaluations are intended to advance evaluators' and clients' general understanding of their organizations. In these cases focused, practical information is less important than model-building. Immediate decisions, policy changes, and procedural shifts are not intended to result, but a long-term gain in performance within the evaluated organization is anticipated as an outcome of improved planning. An example is the linking of various indices of organizational performance in a causal model, so that changes in one can be used to predict changes in others. Criteria for success would include (1) sampling procedures appropriate for generalization within the organization; (2) reliable and valid measures; (3) appropriate statistical analyses; (4) results relevant for planning; (5) relevance grasped by clients; and (6) improvement in planning in areas related to the study.

Although the primary mission of human service evaluators is to provide internally useful information, external audiences can be important as well. This concerns not who the clients are for evaluations, but rather where evaluators expect changes to take place as a result of their work. When the intended sites for impact range beyond the site of the evaluation, the purposes of the evaluator include generalizability of findings. We have acknowledged this by creating a dimension orthogonal to decision relevance to represent locus of intended impact. As the following brief descriptions show, external impacts also can be ranged along a continuum of decision relevance.

Evaluation done with the purpose of influencing major decisions in other organizations is readily illustrated by the kind of summative study intended to promote adoption of an innovative service program in other settings. A thoroughly rigorous design with special attention to external validity is a prime criterion in this case. All of the concerns expressed in the literature on effective dissemination also may be applied as criteria—of particular relevance is the choice of a medium for reaching the proper audience; that is, those who have the most influence on decisions to adopt new programs. Evaluations may not be intended to lead to major changes in other organizations, but may be done with the purpose of demonstrating the value of technical or procedural innovations. In the latter case less emphasis is likely to be placed on design rigor than in the former one, but a similar concern for effective dissemination should be present. Occasionally, an evaluation may be done with the generation of exportable norms for some performance index as one object. In such a case, it is important to use objective and unbiased measures of the appropriate aspects of performance and to report them clearly to the external body which will make use of the data.

Most familiar to academically based social scientists is the use of evaluation to expand the frontiers of scientific knowledge. No immediate relevance to organizational functioning is necessary. The appropriate criteria for metaevaluation are those which would be applied to any effort to provide generalizable knowledge and/or methodological advances in a science. Acceptance for publication in a reputable journal would be prime evidence of good quality as judged by professional colleagues.

The matrix described above captures the variety of purposes for evaluation which are likely to be openly acknowledged by the evaluator and clients for an evaluation. At the risk of tarnishing the elegance of our model, we feel it necessary to add a final cluster of "local" purposes which are covert in nature. As has been noted, such purposes may be intended by both evaluators and clients. Examples include (1) attempts to expand, maintain, undermine, or control the power of individuals or groups within the organization; (2) efforts to produce compromise between warring forces.; (3) attempts to enhance prestige or displace blame; and (4) attempts to provide legitimacy for a decision which has been made but not announced, or to postpone a decision which is painful. In such cases the only available criterion is a subjective judgment of the extent to which such purposes were fulfilled.

When evaluators wish to examine the extent to which an evaluation project has succeeded in accomplishing its objectives, they are concerned not only with their own perspective, but also with the views of key clients. In some situations there may be complete harmony among clients and evaluators as to purposes and results of an evaluation. However, it appears unwise to assume such harmony, and useful metaevaluative feedback entails a parallel review of purposes, and success in accomplishing them, by relevant clients. During the planning of an evaluation, evaluators frequently must identify and integrate the conflicting purposes of several clients, as well as their own. Experience suggests that multiple studies under one title, false advertising about benefits from evaluation, and intentionally abortive evaluation attempts are common solutions to the problem. The proposed model can be used to clarify the issues, but it does not resolve the problem. Once an evaluation has been completed, a weighted averaging approach can be used to estimate overall success from the standpoint of the evaluator, with weights assigned to clients in terms of their relative significance to the evaluator (for example, in terms of their power and willingness to act on the results in combination with their direct control over the evaluator's budget).

On the basis of the above schema, it is possible to characterize a specific evaluation project in terms of its intended consequences, to list the chief clients for the results, and to represent the extent to which the project has achieved the purposes intended by the evaluator and various clients. These purposes can be further subdivided along a means-end continuum. In the following sections some remaining concerns for metaevaluators will be reviewed.

UNINTENDED CONSEQUENCES

In addition to intended purposes, both covert and overt, an evaluation activity may have unintended consequences, and these can be acknowledged in retrospect in determining the usefulness of the evaluation. These may be both positive and negative consequences and sometimes may have little to do with the content of a final report of the evaluation. When administrators and staff anticipate the implementation of an evaluation of their organization or program, they may change their performance in a desirable direction before any data are collected. Evaluated personnel may become so fearful of or hostile toward the evaluation enterprise that the present data and future studies are seriously jeopardized. Decision makers may misinterpret or overinterpret reported evaluation results, seeing what they wish to see or genuinely misunderstanding the facts as reported.

COSTS

The foregoing explication has consistently reflected our concern with the actual utility of evaluation as it is conducted on an ongoing basis within human service organizations. Along with Stufflebeam (1974), we acknowledge that the cost of evaluation must be taken into account as well. A straightforward approach to the calculation of costs would include staff time (salary and fringes), equipment costs, computer time, overhead, and dissemination costs. Many evaluators may be disturbed at the prospect of applying such frighteningly crude cost-effectiveness standards to themselves. However, in addition to the obvious fairness of such an application, given its frequent employment by us with other targets, the costs of alternative evaluation strategies can be used formatively by evaluators to improve their own efficiency before administrators step in with more Draconian measures.

CONVERGENCE OF MULTIPLE METHODS

The above proposal represents a thorough cataloging of the variety of aspects of human service evaluation which might be taken into account in judging merit and providing feedback to improve evaluation effectiveness. Throughout the discussion the impression has been given that the evaluator, and some primary clients, can make judgments on the many proposed criteria, and that these judgments in turn can be quantified and combined to yield metaevaluative profiles. While we do aspire to this level of analysis, we are still moving toward it. In order to validate the approach, other convergent sources of information should be explored whenever possible.

Because of their continuing role within an organization, many evaluators have other evidence about evaluation impact which can be used to substantiate the judgments they and their clients have made. One of these is the written policy of the organization. Additions, deletions, and modifications in formal policy can be linked to evaluation projects which have preceded and followed them. Objective tallies of this sort can be compared to subjective judgments of impact. However, there are difficulties with this approach: it is our experience that policy changes may be formally updated only in the flurry of preparation that takes place prior to accreditation visits or in response to similar cyclic external pressures. As a result, the temporal link between evaluation and managerial response may be obscured.

A second means of validating subjective measures of evaluation impact is also made possible by the continuing presence of the evaluator in the setting. When policy or procedural recommendations have been made and followed, continued monitoring or a restudy can document the extent to which the evaluator's intervention has led to desired organizational changes. Note that the hope is *not* to replicate a prior finding, but to find changes from a previous study in a desired direction. Restudy may seem an obvious means of establishing the merit of some kinds of evaluations, but the expenditure of time and money involved in such efforts militates against their frequent occurrence. In addition, this kind of metaevaluation suffers from all the flaws of the classic pre-post design.

When a subsystem within the organization is the target for evaluation, a suggestion by Scriven (1975) provides another useful approach to metaevaluation which is particularly well suited to assessing the quality of the process of evaluation. Scriven advised soliciting metaevaluative feedback from staff in the evaluated subsystem. In Scriven's view, such reactions could be incorporated into the final report of the evaluation itself. Our own extension of Scriven's suggestion is to treat evaluatee feedback as formative, using it to evolve more effective future evaluation tactics, rather than simply viewing it as a rebuttal.

Each of these alternative approaches to metaevaluation has certain drawbacks as well as advantages, and the most promising use we see for them is as sources of convergent validation in measuring the several classes of evaluation results. Our schema can serve as a checklist of possible results, for each of which one or more specific measures can be devised. Or it can stand in its own right as a means for evaluators and clients to proclaim their intentions and judge the results of individual evaluation projects.

Behind our proposal for metaevaluation tactics in the human services lies a more general concern for a self-critical stance on the part of evaluators. We believe there is a need for more than hand-wringing about the frequent failure of evaluation to affect managerial action, and we believe the typical role of the human service evaluator provides an especially supportive context for formative metaevaluation. Although the daily pressures of the role may seem to make metaevaluation a luxury, we believe the survival of the evaluation enterprise as a meaningful contribution to organizational effectiveness is contingent on genuine efforts along the lines we have suggested.

REFERENCES

BENNETT, C. A. and A. LUMSDAINE (1975) "Social program evaluation: Definitions and issues." In C. A. Bennett and A. A. Lumsdaine (eds.) Evaluation and Experiment. New York: Academic Press.

BROWN, R. D., L. A. BRASKAMP and D. L. NEWMAN (1978) "Evaluation credibility as a function of report style." Evaluation Quarterly 2:331-341.

COHEN, L. H. (1977) "Factors affecting the utilization of mental health evaluation research findings." Professional Psychology 8:526-534.

COOK, T. D. and C. L. GRUDER (1978) "Meta-evaluation research." Evaluation Quarterly 2:5-51.

COURSEY, R. D. (1977) "Basic questions and tasks." In R. D. Coursey, G. A. Specter, S. A. Murrell, and B. Hunt (eds.) Program Evaluation for Mental Health. New York: Grune and Stratton.

DAVIS, H. R. and S. E. SALASIN (1975) "The utilization of evaluation." In E. L. Struening and M. Guttentag (eds.) Handbook of Evaluation Research (Vol. 1). Beverly Hills, CA: Sage.

FAIRWEATHER, G. W., D. H. SANDERS, and L. TORNATZKY (1974) Creating Change in Mental Health Organizations. New York: Pergamon.

HARGREAVES, W. A., C. C. ATTKISSON, and F. M. OCHBERG (1977) "Outcome studies in mental health program evaluation." In W. A. Hargreaves, C. C. Attkisson, and J. E. Sorenson (eds.) Resource Materials for Community Mental Health Program Evaluation (DHEW pub. #ADM77-328). Washington, DC: U.S. Government Printing Office.

HIRI [Human Interaction Research Institute] (1976) "Putting knowledge to use: A distillation of the literature regarding knowledge transfer and change." Washington, DC: National Institute of Mental Health.

LUND, D. A. (1978) "Mental health program evaluation: Where do you start?" Evaluation and Program Planning 1(1):31-40.

McINTYRE, M. H., C. C. ATTKISSON, and T. W. KELLER (1977) "Components of program evaluation capability in community mental health centers." In W. A. Hargreaves, C. C. Attkisson, and J. E. Sorenson (eds.) Resource Materials for Community Mental Health Program Evaluation (DHEW pub. #ADM77-328). Washington, DC: U.S. Government Printing Office.

MECHANIC, D. (1975) "Evaluation in alcohol, drug abuse, and mental health programs: Problems and prospects." In J. Zusman and C. R. Wurster (eds.) Program Evaluation: Alcohol, Drug Abuse, and Mental Health Services. Lexington, MA: D. C. Heath.

MURRELL, S. A. (1976) "Selected conversion techniques for program evaluation." Presented at Region 1 Program Evaluation Conference, Providence, Rhode Island.

——— and F. BROWN (1977) "Judging program evaluations: Criteria in contexts." In R. D. Coursey, G. A. Specter, S. A. Murrell, and B. Hunt (eds.) Program Evaluation for Mental Health. New York: Grune and Stratton.

SCHULBERG, H. C. and F. BAKER (1969) "Program evaluation models and the implementation of research findings." In H. C. Schulberg, A. Sheldon, and F. Baker, Program Evaluation in the Health Fields. New York: Behavioral Publications.

SCRIVEN, M. S. (1975) "Evaluation bias and its control." Kalamazoo, MI: Western Michigan University Evaluation Center.

——— (1969) "An introduction to meta-evaluation." Educational Product Report 2: 36-38.

——— (1967) "The methodology of evaluation." In Perspectives of Curriculum Evaluation (AERA monograph series on curriculum evaluation, No. 1). Chicago: Rand-McNally.

STUFFLEBEAM, D. L. (1978) "Meta-evaluation: an overview." Evaluation and the Health Professions 1.

——— (1974) "Meta-evaluation." Kalamazoo, MI: Western Michigan University Evaluation Center.

WEISS, C. H. (1973) "Where politics and evaluation research meet." Evaluation 1:37-45.

WINDLE, C. (1976) "A crisis for program evaluation: An embarrassment of opportunity." Presented at the Region I Program Evaluation Conference, Providence, Rhode Island.

4

Raymond W. Carlson
Dalhousie University

POURING CONCEPTUAL FOUNDATIONS:
A Utilization Role and Process
for Evaluation Research

Evaluation research has experienced rapid development with consequent diversification in purpose, methods, and roles. Such diffusion muddles communication, particularly as individuals with differing perspectives become involved. At the current time it seems possible to summarize such perspectives into three categories:

(1) *Accreditation.* A concern with comparing a program or program elements to a defined set of standards with the underlying issue being fairness.
(2) *Research.* A concern with knowledge-building through control of the variables involved, with the underlying issue being accuracy.
(3) *Planning.* Improving the comprehensiveness, accuracy, and relevancy of the information available for decision-making at the funding, administrative, and service delivery levels, with the underlying issue being improved decisions.

Each of these traditions offers a particular contribution, but is inadequate if isolated from the other two. Standard setting can improve the equity of pressured judgments, but risks strengthening traditions that may be biased away from effectiveness. Research prioritizes caution and accuracy, but tends to be limited in comprehensiveness and responsiveness. Planning expands understanding of decisions to be made, but cannot offer confident causal explanations. In other words, each of these traditions requires the challenges produced by the other two. The evaluation research field, however, in its own need for identity, tends to seek one tradition, thus forcing these alternatives into conflicted jealousy. The Evaluation Research Society, in entitling its annual meeting "Pluralism in Evaluation," seems to be moving away from such preoccupation with uniformity.

The following presentation emphasizes a planning orientation and thus relies on the respondent's willingness to react within this planning context. Such a context may have been best summarized when Cronbach (1977) suggested at the first Evaluation Research Society annual meeting that the test of an evaluation is whether the system functions better as a result of the evaluation effort.

A BASIS FOR IMPROVED UTILIZATION

Utilization has been evaluation's weakest link. The process outlined in this presentation assumes that the *basic obstacle to utilization is the conceptual preparation of the management personnel involved.* Administrators and service delivery staff cannot be expected to be highly rational; they are caught in a pressured situation that demands responsiveness more than clarity, relationships and connections more than effectiveness. Rein and Schon (1977) suggest that the issue is "problem-setting" rather than problem-solving. In other words, the task is to create a conceptual setting that will help to highlight the alternatives available and the implications of selecting among the alterantives.

Study of *cognitive processes* has produced a variety of theories, but all have been organized around a central assumption: that perceptual senses are constantly bombarded by an array of stimuli too varied and too frequent to be "understood." The function of the cognitive facet of perception is to reduce and organize these stimuli into an interpretable pattern. Such processes most commonly utilize a principle, a visual image, an analogy, or a story line to provide the basis for selecting and organizing stimuli.

The expertise of analysts has been to develop more complicated methods: theories, morphologies, teratologies, matrices, and lattices. The more complicated the model, the more necessary it is to systematize development, testing, and application rather than relying on spontaneous recollection alone. At base, the issue is that the human mind cannot handle the complexity with which it is faced; thus, the easiest alternative is to grossly oversimplify the world. In order to maintain a more complex reality, it is necessary to accept systematic use of conceptual models as a replacement for a sense of personal cognitive control.

Developing any models is inhibited by the nature of management. Mintzberg (1975) reviewed research, including his own, on the behavior of managers in business. He suggests that their actions are necessarily superficial, intuitive, and ambiguous. He relates this behavior to the number of short-term, verbal and other-initiated contacts managers experience. The resultant pattern of decision-making has been summarized as "satisficing," a term coined by Herbert Simon to suggest trying to satisfy the clearest or most threatening pressures without necessarily exceeding pressure reduction. In an unstable environment, this pattern becomes management by crisis.

Research is more of a hindrance than an aid to the harried manager. Cohen and Weiss (1977) reviewed the research on race and public schools. Focusing on policy implications, they note that as more research was demanded in order to resolve the question, the actual effect was reversed. Each new project tended to complicate interpretation by demonstrating that current assumptions were inadequate. It is not surprising that the manager, preoccupied with pressures and presented with "complexifying" research findings, discovered some method to ignore the research.

Hawkins (1978) notes several studies in addition to Mintzberg's in which managerial decision makers demonstrated a preference for information derived from informal, verbal contact rather than written reports or even direct observation. Such a pattern allows simplification because of its emphasis on reputation, but also allows gauging the emotional fervor of reactions. Such emotional content is particularly valuable for the satisficing pattern referred to above.

The typical alternative to satisficing is that of *optimizing*—that is, seeking to do as well as possible. The decision-making implication of optimizing is the need to unequivocally identify the best solution. Ackoff (1970) suggests a third alternative labeled "adaptivizing." He points out that optimization is not useful in areas where predictiveness is low or ignorance is high. In the former case developing a plan with clearly specified contingencies is important, whereas in the latter case preparation for responsiveness is necessary. With this need for flexibility, the emphasis in adaptivizing is on the process of planning rather than the product.

Involvement of the potential decision makers is essential to utilize their insights, but also to spur interest and respect in an effort to complexify decision-making. Another key ingredient is concern for building decisions around the natural potential of the situation, building on the motivations and values of the people involved, and seeking superordinate goals—in other words, adapting the organization to its own potential. An overriding goal is to create an aura of organizational competence, both to help internal staff avoid preoccupation with mistakes and to seek status externally to reduce the need for seeking continual appeasement. Traditional management requires continual seeking of soft information on current prejudices or perspectives of those responsible for the survival or growth of the program. Only those programs that establish a reputation for leadership and competence have escaped this necessity.

The locus of Ackoff's system is an individual or group responsible for determining, organizing, and testing expectations about program performance and impacts. Management staff are too pressured to take on this responsibility; they can provide their expectations and projections, but a separate role is required to build these estimates and other available information into complex models, to identify implications, and to arrange for testing key assumptions. The manager remains responsible for the decisions, but with more awareness of alternatives, subtle implications, and any discrepancies between expectations and data collected.

The above comments are intended to suggest that evaluation staff become responsible for a decision clarification process. The basic competencies required are understanding of organizational decision-making, expanding conceptual models, aggregating alternative perspectives, and developing reliable data collection procedures concerning key assumptions. As research on utilization of evaluative data expands, it provides principles for these areas of primary competence. More recent studies have focused on governmental employees. Caplan (1975) and Weiss (1977) supply prime examples; their results seem to suggest that utilization is greatest when the results are discrepant with some expectations but in directions that are compatible with the model's basic assumptions. Another important point from their combined conclusions is that the data-collection methodology should be viewed as trustworthy, a criteria influenced by the background expertise on methodology of the manager involved. Of course, Caplan also notes that the quality or character of the research cannot substitute for the social responsibility of the manager involved—without such responsibility any data becomes another tool for manipulation.

Development of a conceptual "problem-setting" process is not a new concept for evaluation research. Guttentag (Edwards et al., 1975) used Edwards' Multi-Attribute Utility Measurement to aggregate assumptions about a program area into a matrix model. The approach being discussed in this presentation starts at a different point. Rather than seeking a definitive answer on a "best" program direction, the current approach emphasizes structuring a more extended range of projections to identify implications rather than an answer. In addition, this approach is concerned with an interactive, ongoing process of projections and feedback and will sacrifice immediate resolution to insure testing of expectations.

Wholey (1976) proposed aiding managers in developing a rhetorical or summarizing type of model. From this initial effort a more controlled (and thus a more evaluable) model is evolved. Concern is evidenced that the program should move in the better-defined and more valuable direction. The current approach is less concerned with a totally consistent model that is evaluable; this approach suggests that testing focus on individual assumptions rather than the total model. Wholey's model also tends to emphasize the adequate implementation and flow of the program. The current model intentionally separates objectives or outcomes to insure a more comprehensive consideration of the basis for the program.

The Proposed Model:
Basic Structure and Process

Human services tend to provide unique problems for model construction. The most extensive problem is the field's limited experience in such conceptual activity, particularly in relation to outcomes or noneconomic utilities. Table 1 provides an example of a set of questions that might provoke a model of a service program. For organizational purposes the model is divided into three sections: the political context involved, feasibility expectations, and outcome expectations. This separation insures adequate consideration of all three, since greatest experience tends to be with performance or feasibility issues.

The political context is considered by identifying individuals, groups, or current policies likely to influence enthusiasm for or restrictions on a particular programmatic mission. An attempt is made to project the sense of mission or constraints on that mission that might provoke action from each identified source. A mission is usually framed in the sense of a desired change in the status and/or functioning of (a) target group(s).

Assessment of program alternatives relies on identification of a reasonably comprehensive list. Although initially more general alternatives might be considered, assessments have been facili-

Table 1: Questions Used to Frame a Model of Human Service Programs

I. Identifying a Constrained Mission Supportable in the Political Environment:

Consider each of the potential sub-groups likely to influence program development decisions using categories listed below. For each category, list what that group might expect of the program for the five areas noted. Omit if no expectations are known. List in order of priority if more than one expectation.

DECISION INFLUENCERS	(1) Expected Target Population(s)	(2) Expected Benefits to That Target	(3) Expected Benefits For Self	(4) Constraints on the Program	(5) Distinguishing Characteristics of A Quality Program
Those with Responsibility for Decision					
Those Whose Opinion is Likely to be Sought					
Those Who Could Veto Decision					
Staff					
Target Group(s)					
Other Policies, Laws, etc. with Indirect Influence					
SUMMARY OF COMMON ELEMENTS					

II. Assessing Program Alternatives - Feasibility

List all program alternatives assessing each for the areas listed. Begin with broader program categories. Repeat with more specific alternatives for those with highest ratings.

Program Alternatives	Duplication of Other Programs	Accessibility Complications	Acceptibility Complications	Program Flow Complications	Resources Required	Rating Summing Feasibility

61

Table 1 (Continued)

II. Assessing Program Alternatives - Feasibility -- Cont.

Program Alternatives	Duplication of Other Programs Complications	Accessibility Complications	Acceptibility Complications	Program Flow Complications	Resources Required	Rating Summing Feasibility

III. Assessing Program Alternatives - Impact
Continue with program alternatives high on feasibility, and rate each such alternative.
Consider the likely baseline situation for target group members entering the program.
Identify realistic projections of progress on the benefits listed above - I (2), on other individual needs, in developing negative side effects, and in demonstrating the quality characteristics suggested above - I (5). Summarize these effects into a general impact rating.

Program Alternatives	Outcome Re Benefits-I(2)	Progress w/ Indiv. Needs	Probable Negative Side Effects	Appearance of Quality re I(5)	Rating Summing Impact

tated by moving toward the level of program units included in the United Way's UWASIS II (1976). The initial assessment focuses on feasibility: that is, factors that may particularly hinder or support program implementation. A general feasibility rating is used to clarify priorities, but without decision-making implications. Finally, the assessment shifts to impact within the context of the expectations for benefits and quality suggested in the first section, I(2) and I(5). As other areas of impact, consideration is given to progress in relation to the more individualistic goals that motivate service usage and to possible side-effects, such as the effects on a client's family, community, or employer. Causal explanations of outcome are neglected in favor of projections of likely impact. As Spillerman (1975) notes in relation to social forecasting, it is more realistic to project such expectations based on past trends and/or general structural influences than to seek a model able to completely explain interactional causation.

This set of questions offers only a structure to expand comprehensiveness. Filling it in requires a complex process to identify and aggregate expectations from anyone with a stake in the decision or with a useful perspective. Also problematic is the need to compensate for potential unpreparedness to express expectations. The following steps present an example of a process for generating a model of a service. These facets are neither the only approach nor an adequate road map.

Step 1. Potential participants will tend to include management and supervisory personnel, planners, service delivery staff, and referral sources. In the first two categories the individual necessarily tends to develop a set of assumptions about the services involved. As a result, such assumptions can be identified by soliciting reactions and extensions to a sample model generated from Table 1. In the latter two categories, however, individuals tend to have difficulty with such general questions, probably because of a tendency to be situationally responsive.

The Goal and Service Progress Record shown in Table 2 is an example of a way to generate assumptions on a case-by-case

Table 2: Goal and Service Progress Record

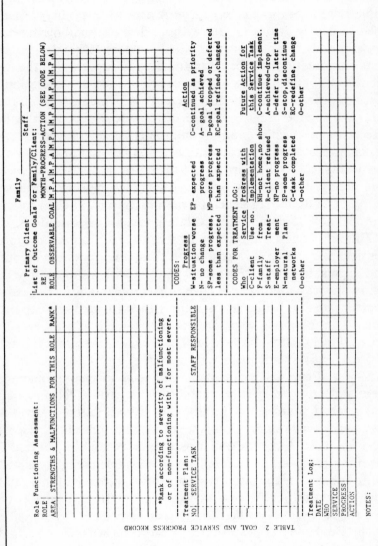

TABLE 2 GOAL AND SERVICE PROGRESS RECORD

Primary Client _____ Family _____ Staff _____

Role Functioning Assessment:

ROLE AREA	STRENGTHS & MALFUNCTIONS FOR THIS ROLE	RANK*

*Rank according to severity of malfunctioning or of non-functioning with 1 for most severe.

Treatment Plan:

NO.	SERVICE TASK	STAFF RESPONSIBLE

List of Outcome Goals for Family/Client:

RE ROLE	OBSERVABLE GOAL	MONTH-PROGRESS-ACTION (SEE CODE BELOW) M P A M P A M P A M P A M P A M P A

CODES:

Progress
W-situation worse   EP- expected progress
N- no change
SP-some progress, MP-more progress
less than expected   than expected

Action
C-continued as priority
A- goal achieved
D-goal dropped or deferred
RC-goal refined, changed

CODES FOR TREATMENT LOG:

Who	Service	Progress with
C-client	Use no.	Implementation
F-family	from	NH-not home,no show
S-staff	Treat-	R-client refused
E-employer	ment	NP-no progress
N-natural	Plan	SP-some progress
networks		C-task completed
O-other		O-other

Future Action for
this Service Task
C-continue implement.
A-achieved-drop
D-defer to later time
S-stop,discontinue
RC-redefine, change
O-other

Treatment Log:

DATE				
WHO				
SERVICE				
PROGRESS				
ACTION				

NOTES:

basis. This form is completed for each case asking service delivery personnel to:

(a) list the patient or client's strengths and weaknesses in terms of role-functioning;
(b) prioritize identified weaknesses in relation to importance in inhibiting greater self-care and self-responsibility;
(c) translate each prioritized role weakness into observable goal(s);
(d) assess monthly the progress toward each goal;
(e) list all planned treatment or service tasks; and
(f) log each client contact and whether the planned tasks were implemented.

Such records can be aggregated to identify the service model being applied—that is, the concrete types of role functioning weaknesses typically prioritized, the types of goals viewed as reflective of resolution of these problems, the amount of progress that tends to occur for different types of goals, the types of service tasks that tend to be established to achieve different goal *categories*, and obstacles in implementing services.

Feasibility determines the number of individuals involved in completing the questionnaire and/or the goal and service progress records. The intent is maximum feasible involvement of individuals expected to use the results of the process being outlined.

Step 2. The questionnaire responses and service models generated are merged into overall models. As divergence in perspectives is discerned, these are juxtaposed to emphasize the resultant choices. Available research or other information relevant to such choices is gathered and used to help support alternatives or suggest new ones. The model is recirculated to the individuals previously involved. Each point involving choice is distinguished with a request for weighting one's willingness to accept each alternative. Instructions for this weighting process stress the fact that majority points of view may be biased by various types of myths. Respondents are asked to review the basis for their own views and attempt to clarify the soundness of that basis. Respondents are then asked to omit items if they lack a basis for making projections. Also noted is a request to avoid the tendency to over-simplify one's experience by funneling it into a few key causal relationships.

Step 3. A model is developed reflecting those alternatives receiving the highest weightings. If alternatives receive similar weightings, the resultant variations are included. In instances where a divergent view was consistently reflected in the responses of individuals in similar roles or locations, a separate model is generated to identify the differences. The focus is for respondents to be prepared to identify goal-attainment implications of alternative program development activities.

Step 4. The model produced is distributed, and examples of decision implications are noted. A few assumptions are selected because of their central role and because they received contradictory or mixed acceptance. Where separate models have been developed for a particular subgroup, the assumptions that seem most responsible for the group's distinctiveness are included in this list of key assumptions. For each key assumption noted, either as central or as one that distinguishes subgroups, a plan for collecting data to test the assumption is also included. Respondents are asked to indicate whether they would be concerned about the accuracy of such data. Various possible results for the data collection are projected along with the implications for the model. Respondents are asked to indicate how they would take action in response to each projection.

Step 5. Responses to the last distribution are reviewed to tally the likely action implications if different results are obtained through data collection. If a respondent indicates serious doubt about the reliability of the intended data, that person's statement of action implications is ignored. A research plan is implemented to carry out the data collection indicated for those assumptions that were identified as most likely to lead to major changes.

Step 6. The data collected is analyzed in relationship to the projections produced by the second questionnaire. The results are reported, emphasizing discrepancies from previous expectations and noting the action implications evoked through the third questionnaire. These results and a revised set of models are distributed with a questionnaire soliciting indications of changes in the respondents' assumptions.

Step 7. The data collection is continued to assess variations over time or with action changes. Additional research plans are implemented to test the next most significant key assumptions. Eventually, as the interrelationships between performance and outcome begin to be suggested, a new set of basic questions is developed and the process begins anew.

CONCEPTUAL FOUNDATIONS

The impact of this process is intended first as a reorientation. Service delivery and management personnel should practice greater caution about impulsive projections without considering alternatives and potential implications of future change. Additionally, their orientation toward research should relate more to testing assumptions than to giving answers. The need for periodic scanning of the system to identify unanticipated or overlooked obstacles or effects also should become clearer. However, the most important effect should be improved quality of decision-making. Inappropriate decisions based on easing the program's pressures should be less common, whereas decisions based on projected client outcomes should be more common. Testing the accuracy of these intended impacts remains a reasonable expectation and, in fact, a responsibility toward the goal of developing an adequate model of an evaluation process oriented toward improved decision-making and organizational performance.

REFERENCES

ACKOFF, R. L. (1970) A Concept of Corporate Planning. New York: Wiley-Interscience.
CAPLAN, N. (1975), The Use of Social Science Knowledge in Policy Decisions at the National Level. Ann Arbor, MI: Institute for Social Research.
COHEN, D. and J. WEISS (1977) "Social science and social policy: Schools and race." Pp. 67-83 in C. H. Weiss (ed.) Using Social Reseach in Public Policy Making. Toronto: Lexington Books/D.C. Heath.

CRONBACH, L. J. (1977) "Remarks to the new society." Newsletter of Evaluation Research Society 1:1-2.

DELBECQ, A. L. and A. H. VAN de VEN (1971) "A group process model for identification and program planning." Journal of Applied Behavioral Science 7:466.

EDWARDS, W., M. GUTTENTAG, and K. SNAPPER (1975) "A decision-theoretic approach to evaluation research." E. L. Struening and M. Guttentag (eds.) Handbook of Evaluation Research (Vol. 1). Beverly Hills, CA: Sage.

HAWKINS, J. D., R. A. ROFFMAN, and P. OSBORNE (1978) "Decision makers' judgments: The influence of role, evaluative criteria, and information access." Evaluation Quarterly 2:435-454.

MINTZBERG, H. (1975) "The manager's job: Folklore and fact." Harvard Business Review 53:49-61.

REIN, M. and D. A. SCHON (1977) "Problem setting in policy research." Pp. 235-251 in C. H. Weiss (ed.) Using Social Research in Public Policy Making. Toronto: Lexington Books/D. C. Heath.

SPILLERMAN, S. (1975) "Forecasting social events." Pp. 381-403 in K. C. Laud and S. Spillerman (eds.) Social Indicator Models. New York: Russell Sage Foundation.

United Way of America (1976) UWASIS II: A Taxonomy of Social Goals and Human Service Programs. Alexandria, VA: United Way of America.

WEISS, C. H. (1977) "The challenge of some research to decision-making." Pp. 213-233 in C. H. Weiss (ed.) Using Social Research in Public Policy Making. Toronto: Lexington Books/D. C. Heath.

WHOLEY, J. S. (1976) Planning Useful Evaluations. Ottawa: Evaluation Research Training Institute, School of Social Work, Carleton University.

Charles Windle
National Institute of Mental Health

5

THE CITIZEN
AS PART OF THE
MANAGEMENT PROCESS

As the United States has shifted from a participatory to a representative democracy, citizens' control over their own lives has decreased and become more indirect. Toffler (1978) argues that the rapidity of social change and a trend for individuals to identify with subgroups rather than the total population are making government both unresponsive and wasteful. Government is nonresponsive because it fails to perceive new needs; inefficient because it continues to answer needs no longer prevalent. To be responsive and efficient, government needs to know when programs should change in order to remain relevant. Evaluation has developed as a mechanism for obtaining feedback on the effects of a program so that it can be responsive. The simpleminded paradigm of this function is a four-step cycle: (1) a program leads to implementation; (2) implementing the program produces results; (3) these results are evaluated; and (4) the evaluation then modifies the program plan.

AUTHOR'S NOTE: *The views presented in this chapter are those of the author and do not necessarily reflect the views of the National Institute of Mental Health. The author is indebted to H. C. Schulberg for critical substantive and editorial suggestions. Whole or partial reproduction of this chapter by the United States Government is permitted for any purpose.*

Feedback from citizens occurs in the form of fees paid, statements of gratitude or complaint, use of services, litigation, and, for public services, votes for legislators with positions in the service or for taxes. Where there is imbalance in power and information between providers and consumers and when few services are available, citizens seem ineffectual in making programs responsive to their views (Olander and Lindhoff, 1975). Program evaluators have developed "client satisfaction" scales to assess client feedback and often present this information as "representing" the clients. This might be a form of technocratic democracy—it seems particularly offensive in professionalizing a function citizens should perform themselves, and converts potential political participation into a technology. The President's Commission on Mental Health (1978: 264) argued:

> We can no longer afford, from either a treatment or a fiscal point of view, the overmedicalization and overprofessionalization of care. Every problem need not be turned over to a specialist. If the phrase "least restrictive setting" is to bear full fruit it must refer not only to physical settings but to professional intervention as well. "Least restrictive" must come to mean "minimally necessary professional intervention."

This concern should also apply to program evaluation which is basically an expression of individual values as well as technical assessment of program results.

The President's Commission on Mental Health acknowledged that loss of the communal and ethical obligation to assist the mentally disabled "has been perhaps the most devastating and far-reaching effect of overutilization of institutional care and over-reliance on professions" (1978: 264). There is also a communal and ethical obligation to encourage citizens to govern themselves (Laue and Cormick, 1978). This is at risk, however, when professionals control evaluations by determining the values on which assessments are made (in the form of program goals) and control the representation of public satisfaction.

To avoid this risk, it is important to encourage citizen involvement in evaluation. Further, citizen involvement is vital if program evaluation is to improve rather than simply support programs.

PROBLEMS IN PROGRAM SELF-EVALUATION

Having hurried to my moralistic conclusion without describing the logical (and emotional) steps which produced this professionally self-abnegating conclusion, let me focus on why citizen involvement seems essential for the success of the technology of program evaluation. Program self-evaluation frequently fails to be used at all or is used in the highly biased form of program advocacy. This outcome stems from the motivational structure of programs. Managers usually see their primary role of supporting the program best accomplished by pointing to a large public need and a program which meets this need. Needs assessments, then, have become popular. It is easy to identify "problems." By assuming that services can solve the problems, the problems can be considered "needs for services." Note that if the services do not reduce the problems, all we have is problems. There are obvious motives for bias in assessing needs by those who want to give or receive the services. Kimmel (1977) has critically analyzed the vulnerabilities in need assessment technology.

Managers can best argue that services are effective on the basis of hope and selected case examples. Next best are studies which suffer serious design faults, such as no control group or omission of cases which dropped out of treatment. Many public service programs are relatively modest, categorical efforts, oversold to the public as panaceas to huge interlocking social problems. Even effective programs will fall below the rhetorical goals of advocates and messianic staff. Least helpful to managers in the short run is a study on how to improve the program. Should the study find solutions, these might not be feasible, appeal to staff, or apply to future conditions. The solutions certainly take time to implement and even more time to prove their value.

The public requires that managers appear interested in making program improvements and, therefore, that they support honest evaluation. However, benefits from study are discounted so severely by the time needed to do evaluations that managers must put altruism above self-interest to pursue self-evaluation seriously.

Managers are interested in information to convince others that the program is already good and, therefore, deserves funding. To derive such information from program evaluation usually requires editing. Thus, the program evaluator is caught between the roles of program advocate (where truth must be subordinated) and profession-oriented researcher. The profession-oriented research role has strong appeal for evaluators, since they can advance their careers by publishing studies which contribute general knowledge (as contrasted with program-specific information). Managers often are not averse to this evaluator role, since research is prestigious and the managers may coauthor some publications. Managers also may feel that the need to preserve their authority over the program prevents them from using information to make the program operate closer to some of its public goals (Katz, 1977; Kaufman, 1973).

Flaws in an Adversary System

Why shouldn't program evaluation be done for advocacy, letting each program hire its own "evaluator" to make its case, as one expects of lawyers? Simon (1978) argued that the lawyer's professional role of adversary advocate carrying out procedural justice has internal contradictions which prevent realizing the alleged ultimate goals of protecting individual autonomy and dignity. The role of adversary advocate is based on an ideology which expects lawyers to be neutral as to clients' goals but partisan in ruthlessly advancing these goals, leading to stylized aggression which may distort truth-seeking and problem-solving. These principles of conduct rest on two other principles, procedural justice (legitimacy through procedures rather than substance) and professionalism (delegated responsibility to practitioners). Simon shows, for various conceptions of advocacy (positivist, purposivist, and ritualist), how "the practices and attitudes of professional advocacy subvert the norms of individuality [autonomy, responsibility, dignity] in the interest of a repressive conception of social stability" (1978: 33). He proposes, instead, (1) a system of "non-professional advocacy" where personal rather than institutionalized professional ethics would guide the relationship between advocate and client, and (2) changes in the legal system "to enhance the ability of laymen to participate actively, and make legal rules and doctrine more accessible to ordinary citizens" (1978: 140). While program evaluation is far less profession-controlled than law, professionalization does occur (Morell and Flaherty, 1978).

An adversary model of program evaluation also seems inappropriate in view of the power imbalance in the social services and the technical difficulty of measuring program outcomes in the cost-benefit units appropriate for interprogram comparisons. For most small or local programs, little competition exists between those service options which should be compared for program improvement, thus making the adversary model irrelevant. Since most program evaluators are employed directly or indirectly by the programs being examined, having program evaluators function as advocates furthers the underrepresentation of citizen/consumer values in shaping services (Olander and Lindhoff, 1975).

Last, there is no tradition or public acceptance of social scientists dedicated to advocacy as opposed to truth-seeking. As Bermant and Warwick (1978: 389) observed:

> The great irony of any advocacy approach for social science is that it would be effective only so long as its audience did not know that it was in operation. If the public came to assume that social scientists, like defense lawyers, were being as selective as possible in their presentation of a case, public confidence in social science would crumble—and properly so.

EVIDENCE OF CITIZEN EFFICACY

If program evaluation is to improve programs, change is needed in the management system. One change with much potential is the inclusion of lay citizens to represent at least three citizen interests slighted in provider-monopolized systems. The most obvious citizen interest is the consumer, the person ostensibly served. Also obvious, but often ignored, are the taxpayers seeking economies. Least obvious are the community caretakers—the family, neighbors, workers, and industries burdened with people's problems.

What evidence is there that citizen involvement will make a difference in use of evaluation results? Probably the most important evidence is logic. It is reasonable to expect that managers' behavior would change if program support depended on their response to program evaluation results (May, 1976). There is also empirical evidence. Primack and von Hippel (1974) found the federal government's science advisory system relatively ineffectual in educating the democratic decision-making process. On several technological issues

> much of the most important technical advice had been ignored— or worse, publicly misrepresented—by government officials. The final outcome of these controversies was in each case much more influenced by the publicly available information and the public activities of scientists than by the confidential advice given the government officials [Primack and von Hippel, 1974].

Mico (1965) reported that those community health studies which simply "gather dust on shelves" were done by professionals who then moved to other jobs, leaving no one committed to following through. Weiner, Rubin, and Sachse (1978) found in interviews with evaluators in well-known research organizations that two influential evaluations were performed under the special study conditions of (1) special sponsor-evaluator relationships giving the evaluator freedom to act and (2) the attention of a larger audience drawn by the evaluator which pressured officials to act. The National Institute of Mental Health's (NIMH) contract evaluations of the Community Mental Health Centers (CMHC) Program is yet another example. Little use was made of critical studies suggesting changes in the program (Windle et al., 1974) until the U.S. General Accounting Office (1974) and Nader's Center for the Study of Responsive Law (Chu and Trotter, 1974) inserted these criticisms into the public debate.

Most examples of the public's role in evaluations emerge from the public media, not professional journals. Since evaluators seem generally captured by the research model and domesticated by program employment, many examples are of evaluations by nonscientists, such as the courts (Kopolow and Bloom, 1977; Turnbull, 1977; Schwartz and Komesar, 1978), investigative reporters (Clark, 1977; Filler, 1976), and whistle-blowers (Nader et al., 1972).

Citizen-consumers and citizens as alternate caregivers have the most interest in the quality of services; citizen-taxpayers have the most interest in efficiency. However, citizen involvement is vulnerable in being limited to the values of the local program (Davidson, 1976). This is most likely for local service-advocacy groups which believe the best way to improve a local program is to obtain more funds from outside sources. There is little incentive for program economy when funding is external.

MODELS FOR CITIZEN EVALUATION
IN THE CMHC PROGRAM

The Community Mental Health Center (CMHC) Amendments of 1975 impose extensive evaluation requirements, including several specific roles for citizens. One is the traditional role of subject. Centers are required to assess the "acceptability" and "impact" of services on the catchment area residents. The legitimacy and opportunity for citizens to take a more active role are recognized in the requirement that: centers disclose their service statistics and results of evaluations to the general public, and have boards demographically representative of the service area.

The most unusual of these evaluation requirements is that the center

> will, in consultation with the residents of the catchment area, review its program of services and the statistics and other information [required in the center's self-evaluation] to assure that its services are responsive to the needs of the residents of the catchment area [P.L. 94-63, Section 206 (c) (1) (B)].

Research on CMHC Citizen Review Requirements

As part of its formal self-evaluation, the NIMH contracted with the Philadelphia Health Management Corporation (PHMC) to examine the impact of the program evaluation requirements of the CMHC Amendments of 1975. PHMC visited a stratified sample of nine centers about two and one-half years after the Act's passage and found little compliance with the citizen review requirement:

> With the exception of broad involvement in evaluation, citizens and consumers do not participate, except as (a) subjects in evaluation studies or (b) in two centers, on citizen advisory groups which existed and were viable prior to passage of the law. The primary effect of P.L. 94-63 seems to have been to make centers aware that boards must have the opportunity to review evaluation activities [Flaherty and Olsen, 1978: 54].

When asked to choose among potential evaluation activities for citizens and board members, center staff favored channeling information between the center and the community and representing the community and its needs. The least favored activities were carrying out evaluation studies or determining levels of effort or criteria. Center staff and board members identified the major barriers to board members' and citizens' participation in evaluation to be the citizens' lack of knowledge about evaluation (84 percent of respondents), lack of interest in evaluation

(71 percent), lack of knowledge about mental health and center services (69 percent), lack of awareness of the legal requirement for centers to involve citizens (60 percent), lack of resources— time and money (56 percent), and citizen perception that evaluation is relatively unimportant (60 percent). Respondents did not identify limitations of the center or its staff among the more important barriers to citizen involvement in evaluation.

Field Tests of Citizen Evaluation

Reports of citizen-based or consumer-based evaluations are often described as demonstrations, trials, or studies. Such descriptions may be a strategy for presenting observations as important enough to warrant publication, but they also imply that the procedures are not an institutionalized agency function and that the observations lack scientific rigor. In fact, few of these reports assess impacts quantitatively or comparatively (except to occasionally assess the attitudes of those involved); and none empirically contrasts the effectiveness of the citizen/ consumer evaluation and professional evaluations or includes costs for either the service facility or the citizen/consumers. In spite of inadequacies, the frequency of these reports of citizen evaluation indicates their face validity and feasibility. They do not suggest how this function might be institutionalized, or whether institutionalization would destroy crucial motivation.

Among the field tests of citizen/consumer evaluation, especially in assessing mental health services, are the following. *(1) The Mid-Missouri Mental Health Center Evaluation.* As part of an NIMH-funded research project on citizen evaluation, $5,600 was provided to a seven-person citizen team nominated by a community health center's "Citizens Advisory Board." This team obtained and analyzed data on admissions and discharges over 13 months, interviewed center staff and others, and prepared a final report. Hessler and Walters (1975) concluded that consumer evaluative research seems possible and has many advantages. On the other hand, they felt that the need to understand evaluative methods and techniques of data analysis and to develop skills and strategies to obtain data may limit the extent of potential citizen/consumer evaluation.

(2) The PEBSI Evaluation. The U.S. Department of Health, Education and Welfare (DHEW) contracted with the BLK Group to test the use of college students and community people during a summer as evaluators of over 100 DHEW projects of 50 types. The BLK Group concluded that

> PEBSI [Program Evaluation by Summer Interns] was a success. In spite of a myriad of problems, many of them directly attributable to its experimental nature, others due to opposition within HEW and elsewhere to what suddenly became a controversial project, PEBSI evaluated 106 different projects in 13 city and county sites, and showed that college students and community people can make excellent program evaluators [BLK Group, 1970: ii-iii].

Despite this assessment, neither DHEW nor the agencies whose projects were evaluated have adopted this form of evaluation.

(3) Evaluation by Public Health Service recipients. The Health Resources Administration (HRA) contracted with the firm of Miller and Byrne to test the feasibility of program recipients evaluating selected Public Health Service programs. The study was to be conducted in cooperation with the evaluated programs. Much difficulty was encountered in locating cooperative programs. The programs ultimately obtained were two in which most program recipients were themselves professionals; the National Health Service Corps Scholarship Program, in which medical students are the recipients; and the National Health Planning Information Center, in which institutions involved in health planning are the main clientele.

Miller and Byrne recruited a team of medical students from three medical schools in Washington, D.C., who designed, carried out, and reported to program officials on a small survey of fellow recipients. This team chose issues to focus on which differed from the interests of the program managers. Although student evaluators expressed satisfaction and some HRA officials said the suggestions were useful, the evaluation impact on the program is not yet clear. The National Health Planning Information Center study could not be completed. Despite extensive recruitment efforts around a single city, recipient interest was too low to carry on the study. Using recipients as evaluators does not seem feasible when recipients perceive the assessment as having low personal salience.

The contractor concluded that:

> recipient involvement in evaluation is certainly feasible but may not be desirable in every situation. In particular, recipient evaluation may cost more in time and money than more traditional forms of evaluation. . . . Also, it is extremely important to prepare program managers to receive recipient suggestions in a constructive manner. There is a useful role to be played by a neutral third party in these evaluations, to serve as an intermediary between recipients and program officials. In some situations, recipient suggestions might be most effectively conveyed through non-program channels [Miller and Byrne, 1978: viii].

(4) The Florida Consortium study of citizen review of CMHCs' evaluations. Four centers and an outpatient clinic are cooperating in an NIMH-supported study to determine ways by which centers can arrange for lay citizens to participate in an agency's program evaluations by reviewing evaluation results and plans (Zinober et al., 1978). Each center chose a specific type of citizen group to study: former clients, persons with "high risk" demographic characteristics, "key informants" about the community, referral agents, and a subgroup of a center's board of directors.

Each group was organized, oriented, and led to review the center's latest annual evaluation report and make recommendations to the center. Groups differed considerably in the nature of their recommendations. Recommendations often reflected views held before this task was assigned. The former client and high-risk groups used their personal experience with the center for many of their recommendations. The "key informant" group listed more services needed in the community, since these needs seemed most salient for this community which lacked a comprehensive center. The referral agents produced a long, well-organized report dealing with a range of issues and progressing from reviewers' concerns, with reference back to evaluation data, to suggested approaches for the center to consider. Many suggestions seemed aimed at increasing coordination among services. The governing board subgroup made administrative recommendations of little cost to implement, including some in direct response to federal oversight reports or previous issues dealt with by the governing board. This group gave more attention to concerns of the center than to community needs. Groups had difficulty covering the many issues in evaluation reports and in maintaining continuity when meetings were widely separated. The study will next assess the impact of citizen reviews on the centers and by citizen review groups led by governing boards and focusing on fewer topics.

(5) Client Advisory Board Evaluation. Morrison (forthcoming) has described the rationale for using a client advisory board for evaluation and the experience in one clinic. Staff, aware of the need to be responsive to client board recommendations, implemented 85 percent of 109 recommendations. Anonymous staff ratings indicated highly favorable attitudes toward the client board.

(6) Contra Costa County Mental Health Advisory Board Evaluations. Teams of Community Health Services Advisory Board members in Contra Costa County, California, have evaluated community service facilities. These evaluations cover a broad scope of issues, involve large citizen teams, and take much time. They are fairly subjective in approach, being based on a consensus of impressions of the evaluation team members plus data from interviews and questionnaires with clients and information from staff in relevant agencies. The evaluations have had direct impact on the programs studied and, in consequence, the motivation of other programs to improve their own evaluations for accountability purposes (Morentz, forthcoming).

(7) Other forms. Citizen involvement in evaluation also stems from other types of citizen activities. The Pennsylvania Executive Ombudsman Program (Commonwealth of Pennsyl-

vania, 1978) goes beyond assisting individuals to class advocacy. By entering the type of individual case advocacy problems in a computerized information system, trends and focuses of problems can be identified simply as an adjunct of direct citizen participation. The recipient rights complainant system in the Michigan Department of Mental health provides a similar evaluation system based upon citizens' initiations of grievances (Mowbray et al., forthcoming). The State's Office of Recipient Rights both investigates individuals' allegations of rights violations and analyzes patterns of complaints, their loci, and the proportions of substantiated allegations. These aggregate analyses may lead to system correction preventing future deprivation of rights.

Other case examples of citizen evaluations have been described (Borus and Klerman, 1976; Krughoff, 1977; Sorenson and Galano, 1976). However, it is often difficult to determine what conditions produced these citizen activities, whether these activities ultimately improved services, whether they became institutionalized, and whether such institutionalization was more beneficial than costly. Motivation for citizen evaluations (at least by professional supporters) and interest in professional publication are often associated, making the integrity of both the citizen evaluation and the publication suspect. More fairly, perhaps this connection is one of the important conditions leading professionals to cooperate with activities in which they cede some control.

CITIZEN EVALUATION PROCEDURES

Past experience with citizen program evaluation has not been studied carefully. Nevertheless, the distinctive features of this process suggest the following tentative advice.

(1) Citizen evaluations should focus on community needs for service. Initial citizen evaluation efforts should focus on needs assessment for two reasons. First, this activity is of considerable importance for all publicly supported social services.

Determinations about level of public support are usually based on judgments of need, a judgment which combines the extent of social problems and the efficacy of the services. When it is difficult to document efficacy, it becomes even more critical to emphasize the problem's large scope. Second, citizens have their greatest relative strength in performing needs assessment, since their expressions of desire for service have much face validity. Since providers are reluctant to give lay citizens or consumers an important role in determining services, it is important that citizens and consumers capitalize on their awareness of community need by participating in evaluations. Conversely, providers are relatively weak in performing community needs assessments—in fact, professionals' vested interest in delivering services discredits their assessments of the magnitude of service need or makes such judgment suspect.

The suggestion that citizen groups attempt to assess community needs is made with full recognition of this task's technical difficulty and vulnerability to misrepresenting personal or group interests as scientific assessments (Kimmel, 1977). Citizen groups should choose simple approaches and combine census data (Windle et al., 1975) with the views of community residents (Weiss, 1975). Citizens should recognize that seeking community views has the even more important function of informing and motivating residents to support services.

(2) Citizen evaluations should focus on clear presentation of information. A main failing of studies by professional evaluators is that their reports focus on study methods and technical results, rather than on clear statements about the implications the results have for program change. Thus, many such studies are unlikely to be acted upon. An important evaluation function which citizen groups can play to remedy this communication failure is by translating technical reports into understandable language and describing the practical implications.

(3) Citizen evaluations should use community linkages to support action on evaluation's results. Citizen groups, by definition, represent the community and have ties to its residents

and institutions. These ties provide legitimacy and authority. Citizen evaluators should use this power to overcome one of program evaluation's major failings: the low use of results to improve programs. Since public awareness of study results often motivates program managers, citizen groups should plan their assessment strategy with an eye to disseminating results to the community and funding agencies, as well as to the program itself. It may be appropriate to contact mass media representatives and funding offices as the evaluation is planned so that the evaluation will be relevant in format, timing, and content to the dissemination and implementation mechanisms.

(4) Citizen groups should follow up program evaluations to increase use of results. Program change is difficult to achieve, since often many interests are invested in the status quo. If change is to occur, continuous expressions of interest and support are needed from its advocates. In a project to develop guidelines for citizen evaluation (MacMurray et al., 1976), six community mental health centers evaluated a year or two earlier by Mental Health Association affiliates were queried on the impact of these evaluations. None reported significant changes. One reason for this lack of impact seems to be that the citizen groups considered their task accomplished once their report was submitted to the center. Lack of follow-up is not unique to citizen evaluations; the NIMH experienced a similar lapse of staff interest in the results of its categorical evaluation studies of the CMHC Program. A follow-up system of querying managers on their plans for using evaluation study results was tried briefly and seemed to focus managers' attention on the use of results. When the follow-up system stopped, managers' interest in using these results disappeared. Citizen groups have a greater legitimacy than program evaluators to query management on its progress in implementing study results, and by doing so can heighten the study's value.

(5) Citizen groups should institutionalize some (but not all) evaluation procedures. Many service programs would benefit from citizen/consumer evaluation, and evaluation skills and

respect developed in one program area should be transferred to others to make best use of scarce personnel resources. On the other hand, citizen evaluation structures should remain open to new approaches and avoid becoming another bureaucracy intent on its own continuity.

(6) Citizen evaluations should use available information. A large amount of information already exists about many programs which can greatly assist local evaluations. Comparative information on agencies often can be obtained from the federal or state governments through simple requests (although sometimes it may be necessary to cite the Freedom of Information Act). The types of evaluative information readily available can be illustrated for federally funded CMHCs from which the NIMH annually collects data on clients served, services provided, staffing, and costs. The NIMH processes this information into statistical indices and distributions of all centers on these indices. Any center can compare itself to all other centers or to subsets, such as those in metropolitan areas. Centers desiring comparisons with groupings other than those in standard print-outs can request them from the NIMH. Another data set for centers comes from federal and state monitoring site visits. These reports usually are not made available, but would be of considerable interest to citizen evaluators.

CONCLUSION

Wildavsky (1977) has pointed to the double displacement of goals in the field of health care. First, people want good health. Since the results of medical care are uncertain, the client's goal of good health is displaced by the more feasible goal of access to medicine. Second, since many patients want psychological reassurance as much as physical treatment, "caring" becomes substituted for "doctoring." I suggest yet another shift in goals. Since providers define "caring" in ways which may suit professionals more than clients, we might substitute for it the more immediate goal of self-control, wherein citizens are enabled to command technologies such as medicines or health care for their own use. Program evaluation, as a tool for program control, should be used by citizens.

REFERENCES

BLK Group (1970) Program Evaluation by Summer Interns. Report to the U.S. Department of Health, Education and Welfare on Contract No. OS-70-102.

BORUS, J. F. and G. L. KLERMAN (1976) "Consumer-professional collaboration for evaluation in neighborhood mental health programs." Hospital and Community Psychiatry 27:401-404.

BERMANT, G. and D. P. WARWICK (1978) "The ethics of social intervention: Power, freedom and accountability." Pp. 377-418 in G. Bermant, H. C. Kelman, and D. P. Warwick (eds.) The Ethics of Social Intervention. New York: John Wiley.

CLARK, J. (1977) "Inside St. E's," a series of presentations on the Six O'Clock News with David Schoumacher, ABC-TV, WJLA, Washington, D.C., May 16-20.

CHU, F. D. and S. TROTTER (1974) The Madness Establishment: Ralph Nader's Study Group Report on the National Institute of Mental Health. New York: Grossman.

Commonwealth of Pennsylvania (1978) Pennsylvania's Executive Ombudsman: The Governor's Action Center, 1973-1977. Harrisburg, Pennsylvania.

DAVIDSON, R. H. (1976) "Breaking up those 'cozy triangles': An impossible dream?" Presented to the Symposium on Legislative Reform and Public Policy. University of Nebraska, Lincoln.

FILLER, L. (1976) The Muckrakers. University Park: Pennsylvania State University.

FLAHERTY, E. W. and K. OLSEN (1978) An Assessment of the Utility of Federally Required Program Evaluation in Community Mental Health Centers. Report to the National Institute of Mental Health by the Philadelphia Health Management Corporation on Contract No. 278-77-0067(MH).

HESSLER, R. M. and M. J. WALTERS (1975) "Consumer evaluation of the health services: Implications for methodology and health care policy." Medical Care 13: 683-693.

KATZ, J. (1977) "Cover-up and collective integrity: On the natural antagonisms of authority internal and external to organizations." Social Problems 25:3-17.

KAUFMAN, H. (1973) Administrative Feedback: Monitoring Subordinates' Behavior. Washington, DC: Brookings Institution.

KIMMEL, W. A. (1977) Needs Assessment: A Critical Perspective. Washington, DC: U.S. Department of Health, Education and Welfare.

KOPOLOW, L. E. and H. BLOOM [eds.] (1977) Mental Health Advocacy: An Emerging Force in Consumers' Rights. DHEW Publication No. (ADM) 77-455, Washington, DC: U.S. Government Printing Office.

KRUGHOFF, R. (1977) "'Checkbook': A 'consumer reports' for the services." Social Policy 36-38 (November-December).

LAUE, J. and G. CORMICK (1978) "The ethics of intervention in community disputes." Pp. 205-232 in G. Bermant, H. C. Kelman, and D. Warwick (eds.) The ethics of social intervention. New York: John Wiley.

MacMURRAY, V. D., P. H. CUNNINGHAM, P. B. CATER, N. SWENSON, and S. S. BELLIN (1976) Citizen Evaluation of Mental Health Services: An Action Approach to Accountability. New York: Human Sciences Press.

MAY, J. V. (1976) Professionals and Clients: A Constitutional Struggle. Sage Professional Paper, Administrative and Policy Studies Series, Series No. 03-036, Vol. 3, Beverly Hills, CA: Sage.

MICO, P. R. (1965) "Community self-study: Is there a method to the madness?" Adult Leadership 13:288-292.

Miller and Byrne, Inc. (1978) Feasibility of Using Program Recipients to Evaluate Selected PHS Programs. Draft Final Report to the Human Resources Administration on Contract No. HRA 230-77-0132 (November).

MORENTZ, P. E. (forthcoming) "A citizen-conducted evaluation of acceptability: The Ronoh School evaluation committee." Pp. 84-85 in G. Landsberg, W. D. Neigher, R. J. Hammer, C. Windle, and J. R. Woy (eds.) Evaluation in Practice. Washington, DC: U.S. Government Printing Office.

MORELL, J. A. and E. W. FLAHERTY (1978) "The development of evaluation as a profession: Current status and some predictions." Evaluation and Program Planning 1:11-17.

MORRISON, J. K. [ed.] (forthcoming) A Consumer Approach to Community Psychology. Chicago: Nelson-Hall.

MOWBRAY, C. D., J. L. COYE, and D. CLIFFORD (forthcoming) "A recipient rights complainant system as an evaluative and decisionmaking tool." Pp. 86-87 in G. Landsberg, W. D. Neigher, R. J. Hammer, C. Windle, and J. R. Woy (eds.) Evaluation in Practice. Washington, DC: U.S. Government Printing Office.

NADER, R., P. J. PETKAS, and K. BLACKWELL [eds.] (1972) Whistle Blowing. New York: Bantam Books.

OLANDER, F. and H. LINDHOFF (1975) "Consumer action research. A review of the consumerism literature and suggestions for new directions in research." Social Science Information 14:147-184.

President's Commission on Mental Health (1978) "Report of the Task Panel on Planning and Review," Volume II, Appendix. Washington, DC: U.S. Government Printing Office.

PRIMACK, J. and F. VON HIPPEL (1974) Advice and Dissent: Scientists in the Political Arena. New York: Basic Books.

SCHWARTZ, W. B. and N. K. KOMESAR (1978) "Doctors, damages and deterrence." New England Journal of Medicine 298:1282-1289.

SIMON, W. H. (1978) "The ideology of advocacy: Procedural justice and professional ethics." Wisconsin Law Review 1:30-144.

SORENSEN, J. L. and J. GALANO (1976) "Collaborative consultation in program evaluation with nonprofessionals." Professional Psychology 7:541-546.

TOFFLER, A. (1978) "Citizen participation and the future of democratic society." Presented to the National Conference on Citizen Participation, Washington, D.C., September.

TURNBULL, H. R. (1977) "Accountability: An overview of the impact of litigation on professionals." School Psychology Digest 6:46-52.

U.S. General Accounting Office (1974) Need for More Effective Management of Community Mental Health Centers Program. Report to Congress. Washington, DC: U.S. Government Printing Office.

WEINER, S. S., D. P. RUBIN, and T. P. SACHSE (1978) "Pathology in institutional structures for evaluation and a possible cure." Paper produced under contract to the National Institute of Education (March).

WEISS, A. T. (1975) "The consumer model of assessing community mental health needs." Evaluation 2:71-73.

WILDAVSKY, A. (1977) "Doing better and feeling worse: The political pathology of health policy." Daedalus 106:105-123.

WINDLE, C., R. D. BASS, and C. A. TAUBE (1974) "PR aside: Initial results from NIMH's service program evaluation studies." American Journal of Community Psychology 2:311-327.

WINDLE, C., B. M. ROSEN, H. F. GOLDSMITH, and J. P. SHAMBAUGH (1975) "A demographic system for comparative assessment of 'needs' for mental health services." Evaluation 2:73-76.

ZINOBER, J. W. et al. (1978) Personal communications from members of the Florida Consortium. For added information contact J. W. Zinober, Hillsborough CMHC, 5707 N. 22nd Street, Tampa FL 33610.

6

Lee Sproull
Patrick Larkey
Carnegie-Mellon University

MANAGERIAL BEHAVIOR
AND EVALUATOR EFFECTIVENESS

The fundamental assumption underlying most evaluations is that they will be "used"; that is, that they will somehow affect decision-making and improve our future circumstances (see, for example, Angrist, 1975, or Pederson, 1977, for this view. We do not believe that influencing decision-making is necessarily the *only* aim of evaluation. As Weiner and Floder, 1978, observe, evaluation also serves the cause of social and cultural beliefs about rationality; it also provides a financial accounting service; and it may "enlighten" policy makers [Weiss, 1977]). Program evaluations are undertaken to provide information that will support and improve pending decisions or create occasions for new decisions. These decisions may directly affect the substantive design of the program being evaluated or they may be decisions to fund, revise, or not to fund future programs similar to the program being evaluated. In any case, evaluations are intended to influence decision-making through providing decision makers with more or less systematic information about the past performance of a program.

Many have observed and lamented the lack of success by evaluations and evaluators in influencing decision-making (Caplan et al., 1975; Wholley et al., 1970; Rein and White, 1977). Two major classes of problems are usually identified by these authors as contributing to this lack of success. First, there may be technical inadequacies in the design or conduct of the evaluation. Through shortcomings in sampling, instrumentation, specification of control variables, statistical analysis, or other procedures, evaluators produce flawed information and reach suspect conclusions. In these cases it is not at all clear what has been "learned" through evaluation. Therefore, it is impossible for the evaluator to give the decision maker information that is sufficiently reliable and persuasive (in a scientific sense) to be incorporated in the decision-making process. Many of the criticisms of federally funded, large-scale program evaluations fall into this category (Rivlin and Timpane, 1975; House et al., 1978; Smith and Bissell, 1970).

The second class of problems may be called "delivery" problems. Through some process, evaluators may have managed to produce information about past program performance with potential value for decision makers, but they are unable to deliver this information to the decision maker in such a way that it actually will be used. In the extreme case, evaluation results may (1) reach the managers/decision makers after decisions have been made, (2) speak to the wrong issues, or (3) may be incomprehensible to all but the most sophisticated methodologists. These delivery problems are the central concern of this chapter.

Whatever the deficiencies in the impact of current evaluation research on decision-making, an important element of any remedial strategy must be a better understanding of the actual behaviors of the managers to be influenced by evaluations. Evaluators need to understand how managers actually make decisions in order to intervene in decision processes. Although there is as yet no comprehensive and unified theory of decision-making, there is a growing body of work in cognitive psychology and organization theory that investigates actual decision-making behavior (for example, see Simon, 1957; Crecine, 1969; Cyert and March, 1963; Mintzberg, 1973; March and Olsen, 1976; Sproull et al., 1978; Tversky and Kahneman, 1973; Slovic et al., 1977; Johnson, 1978). This work can be useful to evaluators who want their work to be influential.

Because our knowledge is still limited, it is not possible to specify with confidence the exhaustive set of managerial behaviors that evaluators should understand. There are, however, three large and general classes of behaviors whose importance seems self-evident and about which there is currently some theoretical and empirical knowledge. These are managerial attention, information-processing, and decision-making.

The simplest model of the manager as decision maker incorporates these three kinds of behavior. Managers operate in a complex information environment and cannot possibly attend to all the information with potential relevance for them. Hence, the characteristics of their *attention* patterns are important. But simply knowing to whom or what managers attend does not reveal how they extract information from or disseminate information to those sources. Hence, characteristics of their *information processing* behavior are important. But even this is incomplete unless we know how managers use information to make decisions; thus, explicit *decision-making* behavior is also important. The role of evaluators in this simple model is to capture managers' attention and provide them with relevant information that will influence their decisions.

This chapter reviews some of what is known about key elements of managerial behavior—specifically, managerial time allocation, information-processing, and decision-making. It then considers the extent to which prevalent modes of evaluator-manager interaction are likely to be effective, given what is known about managerial behavior. The review concludes by suggesting alternative modes of interaction between managers and evaluators that may be more effective.

MANAGERIAL BEHAVIOR: EMPIRICAL REGULARITIES

Within the past 20 years many decision theorists and organization theorists have moved away from rational actor models of managerial behavior (March and Simon, 1958; Cyert and March,

1963; Allison, 1971; Kahneman and Tversky, 1973). Yet, even today, rational models—in which decision makers with clear goals and enormous cognitive abilities strive to learn as much as possible about their situations and alternative responses to them and then choose that alternative which promises to yield the greatest good—are central to many formal analyses (such as those by economists) and permeate our casual and wishful thinking. This is neither surprising nor necessarily objectionable; rationality always has been a high moral good in western culture. As one analyst notes:

> In common discourse the word "rational" is drenched with normative connotations. It means doing that which is "best" under the circumstances, or that which is most worthy of approval. By implication, any decision which is not held to be rational is thereby condemned [Steinbruner, 1974:27].

One major difficulty with rational models lies in their use as unexamined, implicit descriptive models of how managers actually behave as opposed to normative models of how we wish they might behave. It may be the case that evaluators unwittingly have been using such models of managerial behavior. If so, they probably have preferred to give managers more information rather than less, give it to them later rather than sooner, and give it to them in formal documents in an analytic style. Evaluators can then sit back serenely assuming that managers will make appropriate use of their findings.

Research on managerial time allocation provides a picture strikingly at odds with the picture of the careful, analytic decision maker of the idealized, normative models. The manager emerges as a constantly busy person, turning and turned from problem to problem throughout the day, with no time to think, gather accurate information, or weigh alternative courses of action, and barely time to make superficial responses to complicated problems.

Four characteristics of managerial time allocation, consistent across many different kinds of organizations and levels of management, are important to any positive theory of managerial information-processing and decision-making (see Cambell et al., 1970, and Mintzberg, 1973, for a review of many of these studies). First, managers spend a very large proportion of their day in conversations—on average, they spend 75-85% of every working day talking to people. Whatever it is that managers do, they do most of it aloud. The second characteristic of managerial time allocation is that it is predominantly unscheduled and unpredictable. Managers from all levels of the hierarchy—from first-line managers to chief executive officers—spend only about 35% of the day in scheduled meetings. The remainder of the day is unscheduled and allocated in very short periods to a wide variety of activities. The choppy nature of the manager's time allocation, the third important characteristic, is reflected in the short duration of most managerial activities. For example, education program managers have been observed to change their focus of attention once every six to seven minutes (Sproull, 1977, 1978) and chief executive officers were observed to complete more than half of their activities in less than nine minutes (Mintzberg, 1973). The fourth characteristic is that managers' time is allocated as much by other people as by managers themselves. Education program managers initiate only about 50% of their conversations (Sproull, 1977); chief executive officers initiate only about 30 percent of their contacts (Mintzberg, 1973).

Short, informal conversations are the dominant means of acquiring and disseminating information for most managers. This observation can be elaborated in several important ways.

(1) Communication tends to be local. Managers spend more time exchanging information with people in close physical proximity than with more distant ones.

(2) Communication tends to be casual, at least with respect to subordinates and peers. Managers receive and transmit information in short, choppy, unplanned segments throughout the day. Most of this information is ad hoc; rarely are information-collecting conversations preplanned or routinized.

(3) Communication tends to be personalized. Managers talk to people they know. Managers think and speak in terms of indi-

viduals on a first-name basis; they do not think in terms of job titles or hierarchical positions.

(4) Communication tends to be specific and anecdotal. Managers tell and listen to "stories," short descriptions of what happened in a particular situation.

(5) Communication tends to be idiosyncratic. Managers develop "sources" within both their subordinate and superordinate communities on whom they believe they can depend for reliable information on a wide range of topics. They use these same sources when they wish to disseminate information.

(6) Communication tends not to be highly redundant. If managers are sending information, they tend to tell only a single individual and to ask that person to "spread the word." If managers are seeking information, they tend to seek only until they find the first person with that information. There is very little double-checking with different respondents, even if the information received from the first respondent is not pleasing to the manager.

The importance of the characteristics of managerial time allocation for information-processing and decision-making is further underscored when we examine findings from cognitive and information processing psychology on how people make decisions. The scarcity of attention vis-à-vis the potential volume and complexity of information on any particular topic makes managerial use of shortcuts and heuristics in decision-making inevitable. Most of the relevant work on decision-making has been conducted in the laboratory and not in natural settings directly comparable to the organizational settings into which evaluation information is usually conveyed. Nevertheless, there is some evidence (Slovic et al., 1976) that the kinds of decision-making processes observed in the laboratory generalize to the "real world." Furthermore, field studies of decision-making in natural organizations describe the process in terms totally compatible with most of the laboratory findings (Cyert et al., 1956; March and Olsen, 1976). Much of this work can be organized around two broad classes of processes—those processes by which people construct and modify simple, "manageable" representations of complicated situations and those processes by which people evaluate the probability of uncertain events.

Constructing simplified representations of complicated decision situations or problems appears to be a universal characteristic of human behavior (Simon, 1957). It is important to understand the common mechanisms that people use to do so. One very important mechanism involves looking for "explainable" constructs, often employing simple, inaccurate causal theories in a cultural context (Nisbett and Wilson, 1977), and then ignoring or reinterpreting data that do not seem to "fit" the construct. A version of this process, "creeping determinism" (Fischhoff, 1975), is apparent when people reinterpret past events by focusing on selected aspects and ignoring others in order to "explain" a current situation. People tend to explain away the surprises of the past. In retrospect, Pearl Harbor, Watergate, and the Arab Oil Embargo were highly probable events that we should have expected. This "hindsight bias" severely restricts what we can learn from experience—personal or programmatic.

A second common simplification is the use of general or global assessments of a person (or situation) as a substitute for careful, independent judgments about attributes of that person (or situation), even when an adequate information base about the atributes exists. This process, the "halo effect" (Nisbett and Wilson, 1977), often may be operating in school situations when, for example, teachers ignore the standardized test scores of some students but not of others with the comment that the student is "better than the scores would indicate."

More information is often the last thing the decision maker wants, needs, or will use; both of the foregoing mechanisms restrict information to be processed. An example of the apparent unhelpfulness of potentially useful information in a natural setting comes from consumer research. Jacoby et al. (1976) demonstrated that more product information can overload and confuse the shopper rather than lead to more economic purchases. Not even providing unit prices led shoppers to better choices, except where unit prices were perfectly ordered from high to low (Russo et al., 1975). Further, albeit less systematic, evidence that more information is often more harmful than helpful is found in the checkered history of management information systems.

Once decision makers have constructed a simplified representation of a problem situation, by whatever means, often they must then evaluate the probability of uncertain events associated with the problem or potential solutions to it. For example, the decision maker might say, "If we implement the suggestions in this formative evaluation, how likely are we to achieve the results we want?" Or, "How representative of all my program outcomes is this particular success story?" The ways in which decision makers exercise problematic judgment is a second important characteristic of decision-making from experimental studies.

Decision makers are commonly observed to use several information-processing heuristics in probabilistic reasoning. All have the property that they often lead to inferences that would be classed as "erroneous" by statistical decision theorists. One heuristic, the "representativeness heuristic" (Tversky and Kahneman, 1971), uses information about apparent similarity between two objects or processes to estimate the probable relationship between the two (that is, the probability that object belongs to class X or that process X will generate event Y). In making these rough, intuitive judgments about "similarity" people tend to ignore both prior knowledge and reliability questions on data. On some judgmental tasks this heuristic leads to the "law of small numbers" in which people overestimate the representativeness of small samples or overgeneralize from early results. On other tasks the heuristic leads to extremely conservative behavior; people generate explanations counter to the data and underestimate the power of large samples. In erring either way people appear to be fond of simple causal explanations that can be created and held somewhat independently of data.

In employing a second heuristic, the "availability heuristic" (Tversky and Kahneman, 1973), people assess the probability of events by the ease with which relevant instances of the events can be imagined. Hence, for example, the subjective probability of events that have been experienced recently or that receive a great deal of publicity (such as death by botulism, floods, or tornadoes) often exceeds observed relative frequency (Slovic et al., 1976).

"Anchoring and adjustment" is a third heuristic leading to information-processing errors (Tversky and Kahneman, 1974; Slovic et al., 1972), errors in overweighing or underweighing new information (like that produced by many evaluations). If there is a natural starting point for judgment, such as widely shared preconceptions about a program, new data may adjust that starting point, but the effect is likely to be less than it should be.

There are many other regular human tendencies in information-processing and decision-making that emerge from cognitive psychology (Johnson, 1978). Psychologists are finding, among other things, that:

(a) people rely on decision procedures which are easily explainable and justifiable to others and themselves (Tversky, 1972);
(b) consumers' decision processes are affected more by adjectival than by numerical information (Johnson, 1978);
(c) decision-making behavior is strongly influenced by the amount of available information, information formats, and internal standards (and scripts) held by decision makers (Payne, 1976; Tversky, 1969; Johnson and Russo, 1978; Abelson, 1976); and
(d) the greater the amount and complexity of available information, the cruder (simpler) the heuristics that decision makers will employ (Payne, 1976).

The full implications of this work in cognitive process psychology for evaluators in interacting with managers will become more apparent as that work moves toward a more comprehensive, unified descriptive theory of human decision-making behavior.

Because this section has itself been a summary of several sizable bodies of literature, it is difficult to summarize. In effect, however, there are two major points to highlight. First, managers actually spend most of their time in short, unplanned, choppy conversations. This behavioral regularity in large part determines qualities of the information they most often deal with. It is oral, short, specific, and from known sources. Second, when confronted with complicated decision situations, managers use understandable but not necessarily desirable ways of simplifying their representation of the situation and estimating the probabilities of various events likely to be associated with it.

CONVENTIONAL MODES OF MANAGER-EVALUATION INTERACTION

Both the form and content of the most prevalent modes of manager-evaluator interaction are somewhat at odds with the modal behaviors exhibited in actual managerial information-processing and decision-making. In form, the manager-evaluator interaction tends to occur either through formally scheduled meetings or through written reports. Evaluators and their information are only marginally associated with managers' ongoing information-processing activities. Rarely is it the case that evaluators have very frequent, very short, informal conversations with managers.

The content of manager-evaluator interactions tends to be characterized by general and aggregated features—statements prefaced by such phrases as "On average, . . ." Evaluation reports, written or oral, tend not to be filled with (let alone based on) anecdotes and specific examples. The evaluator's trade is one of seeing general features and trends; naturally these are what tend to be communicated by evaluators in manager-evaluator interactions.

Evaluators are decision makers just as are managers; hence, they, too, must construct their own simplified representations of the complex situations they face. Assuming that evaluators are sufficiently competent in probabilistic reasoning that they do not fall victim to such heuristics as the representativeness and availability heuristics described above, it is almost certainly the case that the simplified representations created by evaluators will differ enormously from those created by managers. Data or features that evaluators ignore as uninterpretable or irrelevant may be at the core of manager's understanding of the program, and vice versa. Information that evaluators provide to bolster their case, if not irrelevant, may simply confuse or overload managers.

These observations about the probable mismatch between manager and evaluator information-processing go beyond the standard dichotomy of managers as politicians and evaluators as scientists. There are features of information-processing common to *all* parties to an evaluation that can lead to misunderstanding. The "culture" from which each party comes, of course, contributes to what information is more or less likely to be attended to and how it is likely to be used. But even first-time travelers to a new land can begin to communicate with the natives if they have a good phrase book, if they respect indigenous customs, and if they don't expect the natives to speak their language.

ALTERNATIVE MODES OF MANAGER-EVALUATOR INTERACTION

If the conventional ways in which evaluators convey information to managers seem ill-suited to prevalent managerial information-processing and decision-making styles, what alternative modes might be more appropriate? (Remember, this discussion assumes that evaluators actually have information of scientific merit and potential practical value they wish to convey to managers.) Some may object that the following suggestions would compromise the scientific integrity of the evaluator, but this need not be the case. Nothing in the following suggestions is meant to imply that the evaluation design should be predicated on how managers process information. Rather, it is that, given a design and results that the evaluator should have some confidence in, the evaluator needs to attend to how that information is conveyed to the manager. Even "null" effects, the most common evaluation results, often are potentially important to decision makers. Effective evaluation does not terminate with a technically correct design, proper execution, and publication of results.

(1) Be around. The difficulty with "outside" evaluations is that managers exchange information mostly with "insiders." An evaluator may never actually become an "insider," but the benefits of the position can be approximated by simply being present and available most of the time.

(2) Talk briefly and often. Have frequent short conversations with the manager. Because managers are constantly bombarded by multiple stimuli, any single stimulus is easily lost or ignored.

(3) Tell stories. Evaluators should always be prepared with a stock of performance anecdotes to illustrate the points they are trying to make. In the manager's view, the specific stories *are* the point.

(4) Talk to the manager's sources. One good way to relay information to the manager is to relay it to those the manager relies upon as sources. (Obviously, the evaluator can also learn from them.) Evaluators may not have access to the manager every day, but someone does. To the extent that evaluators can influence the conversations between managers and their sources by giving the sources good information, they will have passed on the information to the manager.

(5) Use multiple models to convey information. Because it is extremely unlikely that the evaluator and the manager have constructed similar simplified representations of the program, if the evaluator simply "makes the case" using one consistent framework, it will be easy for the manager to ignore the entire case as a piece of "uninterpretable data." If, however, the evaluator can present the same findings from a number of different perspectives, it is more likely that one of those perspectives will resemble the manager's own simplifications. And it is less likely that the manager will be able to ignore the findings. Evaluators

must assume full responsibility for translating results (that is, mapping from the evaluator's model(s) to the manager's model) because managers are busy and may not be actively seeking more information.

(6) Provide publicly defensible justifications for any recommended programmatic changes from evaluation. Justificatory arguments in the domain of public programs are certain to be very different than scientific arguments. If all else fails, employ lawyers, politicians, and rhetorical social scientists as consultants. Tell them what makes sense scientifically and ask them to justify it.

CONCLUSION

If effective, this chapter will prompt evaluators to consider the behavioral regularities and information-processing styles of the managers with whom they must interact. Perhaps some of the above suggestions will be useful to evaluation practitioners who have devoted more of their attention to scientific problems than to communication problems, but who are interested in seeing their findings incorporated into decision-making.

This review has not offered a "theory" of manager-evaluator interaction. A much better, empirically grounded understanding of actual interaction patterns—the successes as well as the failures—is required to embark upon that theoretical journey. Nor has this review offered managers much assistance in understanding what *evaluators* actually do, how they allocate their time, process information, and make decisions. That is another topic.

Most of the time, most people are reasonably competent at task they perform; "failures" in organizations are rarely traced to individual incompetence. But people always have too much to do, and the capabilities for thinking and acting are typically modest vis-a-vis tasks confronted. Understanding the determinants and consequences of behavior in systems where the potential for action is much greater than the time available for action is an important first step in improving those systems. An important concomitant step is for evaluators to derive their satisfaction from salutory effects on the objects they evaluate and to develop an extreme prejudice against evaluation without such effects. Analytic time, like managerial time, is an extremely scarce social resource, much too scarce to produce reports that simply take up shelf space without making the world a different and better place.

REFERENCES

ABELSON, R. (1976) "Script processing in attitude formation and decision making." In J. Carol and J. Payne (eds.) Cognition and Social Behavior. Hillsdale, NJ: Lawrence Erlbaum Associates.

ALLISON, G. (1971) Essence of Decision: Explaining the Cuban Missile Crisis. Boston: Little, Brown.

ANGRIST, S. (1975) "Evaluation research: Possibilities and limitations." Journal of Applied Behavioral Science 11:75-91.

CAMPBELL, J. R. et al. (1970) Managerial Behavior, Performance, and Effectiveness. New York: McGraw-Hill.

CAPLAN, N. et al. (1975) The Use of Social Science Knowledge in Policy Decisions at the National Level. Ann Arbor, MI: Institute for Social Research.

CARROLL, J. S. and J. PAYNE (1976) Cognition and Social Behavior. Hillsdale, NJ: Lawrence Erlbaum Associates.

CRECINE, J. P. (1969) Governmental Problem Solving. Chicago: Rand-McNally.

CYERT, R. and J. MARCH (1963) A Behavioral Theory of the Firm. Englewood Cliffs, NJ: Prentice-Hall.

CYERT, R., H. SIMON, and D. TROW (1956) "Observation of a business decision." Journal of Business 29:237-248.

——— (1974) "Hindsight: Thinking backward?" ORI Research Monograph.

FISCHHOFF, B. (1975) "Hindsight—foresight: The effect of outcome knowledge on judgment under uncertainty." Journal of Experimental Psychology: Human Perception and Performance 1:288-299.

HOUSE, E. et al. (1978) "No simple answer: Critique of the follow through evaluation." Harvard Educational Review 48:128-160.

JACOBY, J. et al. (1976) "Pre-purchase information acquisition: Description of a process methodology, research paradigm, and pilot investigation." Pp. 306-314 in B. B. Anderson (ed.) Advances in Consumer Research (Vol. III). (Cincinnatti: Association for Consumer Research.

JOHNSON, E. J. (1978) Decision making: What we know about process. Department of Psychology Working Paper. Pittsburgh: Carnegie-Mellon University.

—— and J. E. RUSSO (1978) "The organization of product information in memory identified by recall times." In H. K. Hunt (ed.) Advances in Consumer Research, Volume V. Chicago: Association for Consumer Research.

KAHNEMAN, D. and A. TVERSKY (1972) "Subjective Probability: Judgement of Representativeness." Cognitive Psychology 3:430-454.

—— (1973) "On the psychology of prediction." Psychological Review 80:237-251.

MARCH, J. and J. OLSEN (1976) Ambiguity and Choice in Organizations. Bergen: Universitetsforlaget.

MARCH, J. and H. SIMON (1958) Organizations. New York: John Wiley.

MINTZBERG, H. (1973) The Nature of Managerial Work. New York: Harper & Row.

NISBETT, R. E. and T. D. WILSON (1977) "The halo effect: Evidence for unconscious alteration of judgments." Journal of Personality and Social Psychology 35:250-256.

PAYNE, J. W. (1976) "Task complexity and contingent processing in decision making: An information search and protocol analysis." Organizational Behavior and Human Performance 16(August 179b):366-387.

PEDERSEN, K. M. (1977) "A proposed model for evaluation studies." Administrative Science Quarterly 22:306-317.

REIN, M. and S. WHITE (1977) "Policy research: Belief and doubt." Policy Analysis 3: 239-272.

RIVLIN, A. and M. TIMPANE [eds.] (1975) Planned Variation: Should We Give Up or Try Harder? Washington, DC: Brookings Institution.

RUSSO, J. E. et al. (1975) "An effective display of unit price information." Journal of Marketing 39:11-19.

SIMON, H. (1957) Models of Man. New York: John Wiley.

SLOVIC, P. et al. (1977) "Behavioral decision theory." Annual Review Psychology 28: 1-39.

—— (1976) "Cognitive processes and societal risk taking." In J. Carol and J. Payne (eds.) Cognition and Social Behavior. Hillsdale, NJ: Lawrence Erlbaum Associates.

—— (1972) "Analyzing the use of information in investment decision making: A methodological proposal." The Journal of Business of the University of Chicago 45: 283-301.

SMITH, M. and J. BISSELL (1970) "The impact of Headstart: The Westinghouse-Ohio Headstart evaluation." Harvard Educational Review 40:411-451.

SPROULL, L. (1978) "Managerial attention patterns: A micro-behavioral analysis." Toronto: Presented at AERA annual meeting.

—— (1977) "Managerial attention in new education programs: A micro-behavioral study of program implementation." Ph.D. dissertation, Stanford University.

——, S. WEINER, and D. WOLF (1978) Organizing an Anarchy: Belief, Bureaucracy and Politics in the National Institute of Education. Chicago: University of Chicago Press.

STEINBRUNER, J. (1974) The Cybernetic Theory of Decision. Princeton: Princeton University Press.

TVERSKY, A (1972) "Elimination by aspects: A theory of choice." Psychological Review 79:281-299.

—— (1969) "Intransitivity of preferences." Psychological Review 76:31-48.

—— and D. KAHNEMAN (1974) "Judgement under uncertainty: Heuristics and biases." Science 185:1124-1131.

——— (1973) "Availability: A heuristic for judging frequency and probability." Cognitive Psychology 5:207-232.

——— (1971) "The belief in the 'law of small numbers.'" Psychological Bulletin 76: 105-110.

WEINER, S. and R. FLODEN (1978) "Rationality to ritual: The multiple roles of evaluation in governmental process." Policy Sciences 9:9-18.

WEISS, C. (1977) "Research for policy's sake: The enlightenment function of social research." Policy Analysis 2:531-545.

WHOLLEY, J. et al. (1970) Federal Evaluation Policy. Washington, DC: Urban Institute.

Anthony Broskowski
Stephen L. White
Paul E. Spector
Northside Community
Mental Health Center,
Tampa, Florida

7

A MANAGEMENT PERSPECTIVE
ON PROGRAM EVALUATION

During the past decade the emphasis in the evaluation literature has been primarily on methodology and technique. However, recent observers have begun to note the high frequency of occasions when the results of formal evaluation studies are completely ignored by policy makers and managers. Greater attention is now being paid to those factors that affect the utilization of formalized evaluations (Weiss, 1973; Davis and Salasin, 1975; Bigelow and Ciarlo, 1976).

Evaluators—those who know about and actually conduct evaluations—frequently view the potential users, policy makers, and managers as lacking sufficient sophistication or motivation to act on the results. Managers and policy makers commonly call for less jargon and more simplicity in the evaluation methods being used. But the issues related to underutilization are complex and are not likely to yield to any single solution, such as more training for managers or less scientific jargon (Havelock, 1975). The major reasons for underutilization undoubtedly vary from case to case; for example, factors affecting the use of large-scale evaluations for setting federal policy will differ greatly from those affecting the use of evaluation within a small direct-service agency. Attkisson, Brown, and Hargreaves (1978), in a thorough analysis of the problems of making evaluation useful, identified the complexities of organizational life as a major factor. Part of that organizational complexity is the context and style of managerial life.

This chapter provides some views on the evaluation process from the perspective of agency managers, specifically, the top- and middle-level managers of a community mental health center. This perspective is determined both by history and daily events. In some sense, evaluation has never been an unfamiliar process to managers. Managers, to the extent that they control valued resources, are generally aware of their accountability for the use of these resources. Historically, managers have had their own ways of meeting these accountability demands. Only within the last decade has the evaluation process, as it applies to human service programs, been increasingly formalized and quantified. The range of constituencies to whom the manager is accountable and the number and types of accountability methods that are being applied have increased.

Before proceeding to discuss a manager's perspective on program evaluation, it is important to define what is meant by program evaluation as it is carried out in a mental health center, a situation we hope is not too unusual. First, program evaluation is viewed as a primary management responsibility which is delegated to staff specialists only because of the technical training and time requirements. Evaluation is also viewed as an *ongoing and internal process* that assists the manager in making *reasonable judgments* about a program's effort, effectiveness, efficiency, or adequacy (Attkisson and Broskowski, 1978). While it is based on systematic data collection and analysis, it is rarely a research enterprise undertaken for the discovery of new knowledge. The primary purpose of this process is to influence and guide, but not determine, management decisions, policies, and plans. A secondary purpose, one which easily emerges if the first purpose is met, is to provide accountability to external audiences. Greater elaboration on this definition of program evaluation is provided by Attkisson and Broskowski (1978). It can readily be seen that the evaluation process is defined as one that is carried out primarily to be useful to management—in fact, it is a requirement of management! If managers are not using what some specialists call "evaluation," then either these specialists are describing some other process or managers are not doing their full job.

To appreciate the manager's perspective on the evaluative process, it is important to have some understanding about the context in which managers operate, both theoretically and on a day-to-day basis. One way to understand the managerial context is to conceptualize the "ideal manager" as an information processor. The classical literature on management theory depicts the rationalized activities of management as organizing, monitoring, controlling, and planning. Essential to all these tasks is the element of information. The idealized manager searches the environment and collects data from internal and external sources. This data is reviewed, sorted for immediate relevance, and either discarded or stored for later retrieval. A great deal of management time is spent in receiving, analyzing, and disseminating information to others. One of the most critical and limited resources for the manager is the time to *attend to* complex information. While some managers claim that they need more information, many others now say they suffer from information overload and need better rules for selective attention to competing sources of information (Simon, 1973; Janis and Mann, 1977).

Based on this analysis of what idealized managers do, one would generally expect managers to welcome formalized evaluation mechanisms. But the theory of what managers do and the reality of how they go about it can produce some paradoxical effects.

According to Mintzberg (1973), managers engage in daily activities best described as brief, episodic, highly varied, and lacking continuity. The manager is continually shifting roles and perspectives and responding to multiple demands at an unrelenting pace that leaves little time for reflection and contemplation. Responsible for planning, the manager also must continuously assess future risks and probabilities. Given this complexity, tempo, and uncertainty, managers prefer *verbal* to written forms of communication. Verbal communication lends itself to *rapid exchange* of information, mutual reactive adaptation and analysis, probing for subtleties, or speculation about options and probabilities. Cursory but current information is preferred to routine reports on past activities. Managers prefer conversation, brief memos, and opening new mail to reviewing lengthy written reports on issues outside their control. Managers respond best to information that is readily available, relevant to immediate concerns, and reduced to the smallest possible volume of words and figures.

Two factors that probably distinguish most research-trained evaluators from most managers is their differential tolerance for errors and their willingness to take risks given limited information errors and their willingness to take risks given limited information. Managers must and will make decisions with or without data. Evaluators should endeavor to value timeliness and speculation as much as they value precision.

MANAGEMENT AND EVALUATION

Managers in human services rarely have formal management or research training; typically they are promoted from some specialized service technology. Therefore, they have the characteristics of service providers in terms of training, expertise, and value systems. Their traditional values as service providers can make it difficult for them to work with program evaluators. Many clinician-managers are bored by research and statistics; lack of research training coupled with irrational biases against "numbers" prevent many managers from making full use of routine or special evaluation reports. Furthermore, managers easily may feel threatened because their agencies or programs may be found deficient under careful scrutiny.

Within any complex organization the need and preferences for the type or quality of information with regard to such criteria as frequency, timeliness, level of detail, precision, and scope will vary as a function of the level of management (Gorry and Morton, 1971). Front-line supervisors prefer frequent, detailed, and accurate information about individual clients or staff activities. Top-level administrators need aggregated information of broader scope that projects future options and integrates data from multiple internal and external sources. Furthermore, the tempo of the activity one manages will determine the optimal frequency of useful feedback. For example, emergency service program managers need more frequent monitoring aids than do the managers of long-term residential programs.

Generally, the executive director of an organization must integrate information from all internal sources with external information about the agency's shifting and turbulent funding and regulatory environment. The director's wish is for a few key performance indicators that will monitor overall effort, cost, effectiveness, and efficiency. Top management wants program evaluation processes to help identify and recommend practical solutions to major problems.

Middle managers are those supervisors and coordinators who are closest to line workers and who form the link between the front-line workers and top management. In the human services they are directly responsible for some specific operation or program within the larger human service organization. In this capacity these managers are potential links to all other service programs in the organization and are responsible for responding to their program's daily changes and crises.

Middle managers have a variety of conflicting constituencies vis-à-vis program evaluation. They know that programs must be accountable to top management in terms of productivity and cost-effectiveness with regard to organization-wide goals and objectives. At the same time, middle managers must be viewed by subordinates as their primary advocates. In one sense, the middle manager buffers the line staff from top management scrutiny. The middle manager can be accountable to a variety of other subsystems, including the business office, personnel, and medical records. The middle manager literally is caught in the middle and evaluation processes are seldom seen as salvation.

WHAT MANAGERS
AND EVALUATORS CAN DO

While evaluators must adapt to the variety and pace of the manager's world and the complexities of other organizational dynamics, so, too, must managers strive to recognize the potentials of the evaluation process. Agency leadership can do several things to assist and promote the widest possible use of evaluation results throughout the organization. First, the chief executive must articulate an explicit viewpoint or model of the evaluation process within the context of management and organization. This model may range from a simple view of evaluation as only one of several sources of information for management to an elaborate theory that views evaluation as a form of systemic adaptation or as one method of integrating highly differentiated subsystems within the organization (Broskowski and Driscoll, 1978). Second, the chief executive must consider the ability and willingness to use evaluation results in the selection and supervision of middle managers. For example, the executive director can ask middle managers questions about how they plan to evaluate new programs or methods being considered.

Given middle-level managers who can appreciate the potentials of evaluation to improve their programs, top management must delegate to them sufficient discretion and authority. Among other reasons cited for the low managerial use of evaluation, Horst, Nay, Scanlon, and Wholey (1974) attribute the root cause to the lack of adequate skill, motivation, ability, or authority on the part of program managers. Speaking primarily about governmentally employed managers, these authors described most of them as "pseudo-managers" who lack the capacity to control resources which they supposedly manage. To the extent that a manager is a "pseudo-manager," the results of evaluation will have little interest or impact.

The chief executive can encourage middle managers to use the agency's evaluation staff by asking the program managers questions that they in turn can answer only by getting some or all of the data from the program evaluation staff. Middle managers and evaluators thereby become partners in providing information to the chief executive. The success of this approach requires the executive to initiate the process by asking the *program manager* to address and solve an important issue, rather than asking the evaluator to "investigate" a problem within a given program. When this is done properly, the evaluator becomes a valued advisor to the middle manager, not a spy for top management.

Although the characteristics of middle managers and their attendant problems can create tension between them and program evaluators, there is growing awareness that formal evaluation is here to stay and must be accommodated in managerial work. The middle manager and the evaluator must form an alliance, preferably based on a personal working relationship. It is important that the evaluator be perceived as an ally and a friend to the service program. The evaluator can initiate this relationship by regularly meeting with each program manager in an informal manner. The evaluator should spend time listening to the manager's ideas, goals, and apprehensions in a sympathetic manner, one that makes the manager feel that the evaluator is an ally who understands that the manager is pulled from all sides by multiple constituencies. The sensitive and creative program evaluator will be able to offer information that will help the manager build a favorable case with regard to one or more of these constituencies. In this way the manager will begin to see the evaluator as a friend and a resource. The friendly and personal outreach should not be a one-time venture, but a routine process.

The evaluator can help overcome the resistances of middle managers by eliciting their views and opinions and then translating that information into questions that may be answered through evaluation. For example, a manager could be helped to express concern for rapid staff turnover in the following question: "Based upon data on past employees, what do you think are the characteristics of staff most likely to resign from your program within a year of being hired?" Providing answers to vexing questions like this one will win friends among middle managers.

While the chief executive nurtures a closeness between the evaluator staff and individual middle managers, managers at all levels must not discourage the types of evaluative comparisons that need to take place in the process of resolving the inevitable conflicts that will occur among programs and staff. If top management views evaluation as a potential force for integration and conflict resolution, then management will welcome the debates that the evaluation process can stimulate. Program evaluation can help to pull together the divergent components of a multiservice agency by making regular attempts to share among managers the type of information that helps them understand the *interconnectedness* of their program and that ineffectiveness in one program can create difficulties for others. Through the evaluation process managers can begin to develop a *systemic* awareness that will foster better cooperation and a higher degree of service integration for the benefit of clients.

Unfortunately, management frequently foregoes a searching examination of a serious problem in the interest of organizational harmony and staff morale. In human service agencies staff morale and satisfaction commonly take precedence over program effectiveness or efficiency. The chief executive must nurture a sense of trust among middle managers and staff so that the evaluation process is not seen as a threat to personal security or esteem. The personal *performance appraisals* of staff and middle managers should not be tied too closely to the results of *program evaluation* studies. At the same time, the chief executive, during the periodic evaluation of each middle manager's performance, should explicitly review the manager's openness to program evaluation and demonstrated use of evaluation results in the program's operation.

The chief executive also can serve as a model for others to the extent that the program evaluation staff are welcome to participate in the highest-level meetings and discussions regarding agency policies and plans. The program evaluator must meet with top management on a frequent basis to remain familiar with emergent organizational issues. Evaluators can then demonstrate their utility by anticipating the collection and analysis of data relevant to emerging problems and issues before those problems become crises.

Finally, the chief executive should welcome the evaluation process as it can be applied to the operations of top management. In an agency with a board of directors the chief executive should welcome the board to review and evaluate not only the operations of the individual programs, but the performance of the chief executive. The comparable levels of leadership in government-operated service agencies should welcome the review and evaluation of external groups.

THE EVALUATOR'S PERSPECTIVE ON MANAGEMENT

One of the problems encountered by evaluators is that their perspective can be quite different from that of the management. The evaluator is often trained as a researcher and approaches evaluation questions as research questions requiring research procedures to answer. The manager sees questions as practical and result-oriented, requiring information for immediate decision-making. If information is to be used, it must have potential impact on the immediate demands for action. Information should be meaningful and concrete and lead to definite conclusions.

In presenting information the evaluator must consider the background of the audience. Managers are rarely researchers and few have been program evaluators. Therefore, it is encumbent upon the evaluator to speak in a language understood by the management staff, rather than to expect managers to understand the language of research. Results expressed in technical language can be understood by the manager with an appropriate background, but it is seldom understood by the less research-oriented individual. In such highly technical evaluations it is often a case of too much confusing detail and too little information; thus, perhaps the best approach would be to provide the same basic data through multiple channels. As Cox (1977) suggests, several brief verbal reports of major findings can be followed by a longer written report. This approach is used at Northside Community Mental Health Center. There are routinely scheduled meetings between the executive director and the program evaluator to discuss evaluative information as it is being generated. Individual program managers are generally apprised of the results of studies before reports are written. In fact, they often provide unique insight to data interpretation which otherwise might be overlooked by the evaluation staff.

One of the major functions of evaluation is to provide feedback which leads to program modification and refinement. It follows that much of the resistance to the use of evaluation is a result of the generalized resistance to change that is widely experienced throughout all organizations. These problems are difficult to overcome and involve more than improvements in presentation of results. The cooperation of top management is essential. In addition, there are several things an evaluator can do to help overcome resistance to change.

There is considerable literature concerned with methods of overcoming resistance to change. The classic study of resistance (Coch and French, 1948) suggested the use of participation. Participation by all levels of the organization in the design of evaluation studies can greatly increase their acceptance and utilization. Clinical and middle-management staff can offer invaluable assistance in designing studies through their direct knowledge of programs and clients. If they are made a partner in formulating evaluation questions and design, program staff are more likely to utilize results because the results will be relevant and understood.

The threat of evaluation is most difficult to overcome in connection with programs which are not highly effective. When staff take evaluation seriously they are also likely to be apprehensive about the possibility that program deficiencies will be uncovered. Anxiety can arise when staff members are unsure about the ultimate implications of findings. The implicit or imagined threat involved in evaluation is that punitive action will be taken in response to negative findings. To overcome this problem a great deal of trust must be established among evaluators, service staff, and all levels of management. The purpose of each study should be clearly specified in advance, and the possible ramifications should focus on program outcomes and not on the effectiveness of individual staff members. Finally, clinical staff should be consulted about the methods being considered to conduct the study. When studies are carried out in this manner the imagined threats need not become reality and an atmosphere of trust can develop. Clinical staff should be assured by management that staff jobs and career futures will not hinge on the results of any study. Although evaluation data can be the stimulus for program change when it reveals deficiencies or problems, it is often only one of several sources of data for choosing among alternative solutions after the decision to make a change has been reached.

Another source of resistance to evaluation is related to the low tolerance most people have for criticism. Managers may consider evaluation a personal threat because they see it as a source of criticism of them or their program. Evaluators should be careful in presenting negative feedback. Negative results certainly should not be suppressed, but they can be presented in a diplomatic manner. Furthermore, several small "doses" of negative feedback over time will be more effective than one large "dose." After presenting negative findings, evaluators should be prepared for defensive staff reactions in which program staff try to rationalize the results and attack the validity of the study. Rather than taking a hard line, it is more constructive to allow staff to save face. Suggestions for change can be delayed and implemented in a gradual rather than precipitous fashion. Since the evaluators seldom have authority to enforce change, they seldom are in a position to demand it, even on logical grounds. If change is to be accomplished it must be endorsed by the program staff or top management.

To develop credibility with management it is important for the evaluator to develop a responsive evaluation capacity. A responsive capacity does not necessarily stem from *collecting* a large volume of data. The range of data, its storage and retrievability, and the degree to which it can be disaggregated, resorted, and recombined will determine whether the evaluator will have the information at hand when it is needed. The ability to provide information quickly is a major criterion of an organization's evaluation capacity, and it takes considerable time and effort to develop such capacity. For example, mental health centers are required to maintain elaborate medical records concerning the treatment of each client. However, medical records are practically useless for programmatic decision-making unless they are subjected to a tedious and expensive process of data retrieval and coding. In contrast, the effective evaluator will have ready access to data on type and amount of service units provided to various categories of clients and will be able to integrate these data with data on service costs. The critical skill is anticipating management information needs and in collecting and storing the data in a fashion which makes it readily retrievable and subject to a variety of analyses (Broskowski, 1979). To anticipate management information needs the evaluation staff must remain continuously aware of relevant organizational issues, both internal and external. When such issues are known in advance, data needs can be anticipated and useful information provided in a timely fashion.

Much has been written about the underutilization of evaluation, but little about the problems that can arise when it is taken and used seriously. In a highly dynamic organization the demand for timely information can easily exceed the capacity to generate and process it. Evaluation data then becomes a valuable but relatively limited resource. The emphasis shifts to collecting and storing only the most useful data. Evaluators, like managers, must then begin to manage their own resources and assign priorities to the collection and processing of different categories of information.

SUMMARY

Evaluation is defined as an integral function of management. Evaluation processes must take into account the dynamics of organizational life, particularly the work styles and demands of managers. Timeliness and relevance usually are more critical than precision and completeness. To improve both management and evaluation processes it is important that the manager and the evaluator understand the respective value systems of one another and work toward an atmosphere of trust and collaboration.

REFERENCES

ATTKISSON, C. and A. BROSKOWSKI (1978) "Evaluation and the emerging human service concept." Pp. 3-26 in C. C. Attkisson, W. A. Hargreaves, M. J. Horowitz, and J. E. Sorensen (eds.) Evaluation of Human Service Programs. New York: Academic Press.

ATTKISSON, C., T. BROWN, and W. HARGREAVES (1978) "Roles and functions of evaluation in human service programs." Pp. 59-95 in C. C. Attkisson, W. A. Hargreaves, M. J. Horowitz, and J. E. Sorensen (eds.) Evaluation of Human Service Programs. New York: Academic Press.

BIGELOW, D. and J. CIARLO (1976) "The impact of therapeutic effectiveness data on community mental health center management." Pp. 371-382 in G. V. Glass (ed.) Evaluation Studies Review Annual (Vol. 1). Beverly Hills, CA: Sage.

BROSKOWSKI, A. (1979) "Management information systems for planning and evaluation in human services." In H. C. Schulberg and F. Baker (eds.) Program Evaluation in the Health Fields (Vol. 2). New York: Human Sciences.

——— and L. DRISCOLL (1978) "The organizational context of program evaluation." Pp. 43-58 in C. C. Attkisson, W. A. Hargreaves, M. J. Horowitz, and J. E. Sorensen (eds.) Evaluation of Human Service Programs. New York: Academic Press.

COCH, L. and J.R.P. FRENCH (1948) "Overcoming resistance to change." Human Relations 1:512-532.

COX, G. (1977) "Managerial style: Implications for the utilization of program evaluation information." Evaluation Quarterly 1:499-508.

DAVIS, H. and S. SALASIN (1975) "The utilization of evaluation." Pp. 621-666 in L. Struening and M. Guttentag (eds.) Handbook of Evaluation Research (Vol. 1). Beverly Hills, CA: Sage.

GORRY, G. A. and M.S.S. MORTON (1971) "A framework for management information systems." Sloan Management Review 13:55-70.

HAVELOCK, R. (1975) Planning for Innovation Through Dissemination and Utilization of Knowledge. Ann Arbor, MI: Center for Research on Utilization of Scientific Knowledge, Institute for Social Research, University of Michigan.

HORST, P., J. NAY, J. W. SCANLON, and J. WHOLEY (1974) "Program management and the federal evaluator." Public Administration Review 34:300-308.

JANIS, I. L. and L. MANN (1977) Decision Making. New York: Free Press.

MINTZBERG, H. (1973) The Nature of Managerial Work. New York: Harper & Row.

SIMON, H. (1973) "Applying information technology to organization design." Public Administration Review 33:268-278.

WEISS, C. H. (1973) "Between the cup and the lip—." Evaluation 1:49-55.

Ross F. Conner
Program in Social Ecology
University of California, Irvine

8

THE EVALUATOR-MANAGER RELATIONSHIP
An Examination of the Sources of Conflict and a Model for a Successful Union

Evaluation researchers are becoming regular members of social reform program teams at an increasing rate. The rising demand for documented program effects as well as the increase in the quality of evaluation studies are important reasons why the evaluator's status has changed. This change, however, has not necessarily been accompanied by a change in some of the organizational strains which have characterized evaluator-practitioner or evaluator-manager relationships. As writers in the evaluation research literature have commented, friction between researchers and other program staff is the rule rather than the exception (Weiss, 1972, 1975, 1977; Argyris, 1971; Rodman and Kolodny, 1971).

Conflict between evaluators and either managers or practitioners can be a major impediment to successful evaluation research. The best, most rigorous designs, measures, and data analysis techniques are useless if program personnel refuse to cooperate with the evaluator. Consequently, it is important to analyze the relationship between evaluators and program staff in order to understand the potential sources of conflict as well as the possible methods—both organizational and personal—for precluding or ameliorating the conflicts.

This chapter has three purposes: first, to explore briefly the sources of conflict between evaluators and other program personnel, both managers and staff;[1] second, to describe a recent large-scale program of evaluation research in which the evaluators and program personnel experienced very little conflict; and third, to discuss a model of positive, productive evaluator-manager relations on which this evaluation research project was based. Throughout these discussions we will examine ways in which conflict was avoided and suggest ways in which conflict might be mitigated in other program evaluations.

SOURCES OF CONFLICT IN THE EVALUATOR-MANAGER RELATIONSHIP

Although many writers in the evaluation research field note that conflicts between evaluators and program personnel frequently occur, few writers present a detailed discussion of the sources of these conflicts. Weiss (1972) is a notable exception to this pattern; she has listed six primary sources of conflict (1972: 98-104).

(1) Personality differences. The evaluator is characterized as a "detached individual, . . . cool, uncommitted," and as "marginal," while the practitioner is characterized quite differently: "warm, outgoing, . . . intensely concerned about people, specifics and the here and now." Over the past few years, the number and type of settings in which evaluators are working have greatly increased. Evaluators working in these new settings have needed a variety of different types of skills, both in professional training and in personal style. Indeed, as evaluation research has become more important in policy debates and more visible as an applied social science, the "outgoing" personality type becomes an asset—if not a requirement—for an effective evaluator. The personality disparity between the cool, analytic evaluator and the warm, emotive program staffer, then, probably has greatly decreased.

(2) Differences in role. The program manager is a believer, the evaluator a doubter. The differences in perspectives regarding the program which result from these role differences are a source of conflict. The program manager has instituted the reform effort believing that the reform would improve the existing situation. Moreover, the time and effort involved in moving from conception to implementation of the reform effort tend to strengthen the manager's attitudes regarding the reform program. The evaluator, on the other hand, is more of a doubter who approaches the program without a vested interest in the efficacy of the reform. The evaluator has been trained to be skeptical about the match between the program's goals and its accomplishments. The evaluator questions every aspect of the program, including such aspects as the size and longevity of the program, which to the program manager are self-evident indications of the program's success. In addition, the evaluator does not devote time and energy to the reform effort, so there is less need to justify the effort.

(3) Lack of clear role definition. There may be differences in interpretation by the evaluator and by the program staff of who has final responsibility, control, and authority over different functions. This ambiguity occurs because often there is some overlap in duties and functions of the evaluator and of the other staff members. However, for certain types of evaluation designs, the evaluator needs to make the final decision about which clients will and which will not be served. Unless this type of task conflict is recognized and resolved, relationships between staff and evaluators become strained as the program progresses and the evaluation plan is implemented. Clients can make this problem more salient because they do not recognize differences in functions and so expect and demand direction or services from evaluators which only staff should provide.

(4) Conflicting goals, values, interests, and frames of reference. The program manager or practitioner attempts to provide services to as many clients as possible, believing that all available resources should be devoted to service delivery. Any money and

time allocated to tasks other than service—for example, to evaluation—mean fewer resources for the clients. Evaluators attempt to assess the quality of services provided; therefore, they accept the idea that 5 to 10 percent of the program budget should be devoted to evaluation to be sure that the other 90 to 95 percent is being well spent. These differences in general perspective or frame of reference between staff and evaluator can be another source of conflict.

(5) Institutional characteristics. If the organizational structure is closed, formal, and authoritarian, the evaluator will have a more difficult time communicating with all parties. As a consequence, misconceptions about the evaluation are more likely to take root and are less likely to surface where they could be resolved. Conversely, if the organizational structure is open and informal, communication will be easier among all the parties and conflict is less likely to occur. Apart from the organizational structure, the size of the organization or institution is an important factor in the ease of communication. In a small program, contact between staff and evaluator can occur frequently. In a program which is large either in terms of geographic spread or numerical size, the opportunity for contact and communication between staff and evaluator is reduced and the chance for misunderstanding is increased proportionately.

(6) Aspects of evaluation methods and techniques. Like any other scientific investigation, evaluation research involves the collection of data according to special techniques and procedures. Various changes may be required in program procedures, from minor modifications in routine record-keeping or scheduling of services to major modifications such as special data-collection instruments, new selection procedures for program participants, or formation of control groups. The more definitive the evaluation data desired, the greater is the need for major changes. Any of these changes tend to replace familiar, understandable procedures with those which seem unusual or cumbersome to program staff.

Any of these sources of conflict may influence the relationship between the program evaluator and the program manager or staff. In the case to be described, however, many of these factors were present, but disruptive conflict *did not* result. Following a brief description of the reform program and its evaluation component, some reasons for the absence of overt friction within the program will be analyzed.

THE BASICS PROGRAMS

In early 1974, the American Bar Association (ABA) began a new program in criminal justice reform. The program was developed by the ABA's Commission on Correctional Facilities and Services and was named BASICS, an acronym for Bar Association Support to Improve Correctional Services. As the name implies, the BASICS Program was intended to improve correctional services by involving members of local bar associations in local criminal justice problems. This novel method for effecting correctional reform was developed by the ABA's Commission on Correctional Facilities and Services and the Edna McConnell Clark Foundation on the belief that lawyers and the local bar associations of which they were members were untapped resources in the correctional reform area.

There were several reasons why bar associations were thought to be eminently suited to accomplishing the goals of this program (BASICS Brochure, 1974). Members of a bar association are part of a well-established body and are frequently community leaders. Such influence creates access to the many local financial and human resources vital to a reform effort. In undertaking correctional programs, each association could become part of a nationwide network with established lines of communication, the technical assistance of the ABA Corrections Commission, and the financial support necessary to plan and execute specific, well-defined improvement programs.

The BASICS plan was to activate local bar association members to plan and to implement some type of correctional reform effort. In 1974, the project solicited applications from all types of United States bar associations for small planning grants of approximately $3,000. From the approximately 1,000 state, county, and local bar associations across the country, the BASICS staff and board received 106 applications and funded 80 planning projects in 40 states. After approximately three months of planning, 62 bar associations applied for larger grants up to $35,000 to implement their correctional reform efforts. Twenty "action" grants were awarded by the BASICS Program in late 1975 (Huff et al., 1975).

Because of their interest in effecting "measurable changes" and their previous experience with program evaluation, the BASICS Management Board, the program staff, and the funding agency began to discuss program evaluation at the outset of the program. An interdisciplinary team of evaluators, including a social psychologist with an interest in evaluation research and a sociologist with an interest in criminology, were asked to formulate an evaluation plan.

Designing the evaluation was challenging because it had to conform to the program's unusual operational procedure, which involved two very different stages: (a) the planning phase, during which many bar associations across the country formulated a variety of correctional reform plans, and (b) the action phase, during which a few bar associations implemented very different projects. Because of the differences in number, type, and scope of activity, the research questions and the evaluation plans for each stage were generally unique and unrelated.

The Planning Phase Evaluation

The research questions of primary importance during the first phase concerned the type and extent of planning activities occurring in the 80 locations. Because each planning effort was unique in its focus and requirements, no common objective measure of success could be used to supplement subjective assessments of the degree of successful planning. In addition, specific information regarding these planning efforts was needed by the BASICS program personnel at the conclusion of the planning phase. In a series of discussions between the evaluators and program personnel, two major information needs were identified: (1) a comprehensive overview of the planning activities undertaken by the 80 bar associations (rather than individual reports on each project) and (2) recommendations regarding improvements in the planning phase and useful tactics for implementing reform in the action phase.

A process-monitoring plan of evaluation seemed best suited to meeting these information requirements. These monitoring activities involved a survey of both funded and nonfunded bar associations, interviews with a sample of funded associations, as well as interviews with the BASICS staff and Clark Foundation representatives. Multiple data-collection strategies were used not only to collect the relevant process data, but also to verify its reliability and validity. A survey was sent to representatives of the 80 funded projects and the 26 nonfunded projects; it included questions about the characteristics of the bar association and (for funded projects only) about the planning activities they undertook, the ways they used the grant money, the degree to which they consulted other relevant organizations and groups, and the quality of the technical support they received. For both funded and nonfunded bars, there were additional questions regarding the viability of bar associations as change agents and the priority given to correctional reform work by bar associations.

The product of this phase of the evaluation was a report to the board of directors containing data on the more and less successful aspects of the first phase and recommendations for the next phase (Huff et al., 1975). It is noteworthy that a substantial part of one board meeting was devoted to a discussion of these findings and recommendations.

The Action Phase Evaluations

The primary research question for the second phase concerned the effectiveness of the action projects. Although 20 bar associations were funded to implement correctional reform projects, the projects were so diverse in nature and objectives that no single evaluation design was suited to all projects. In addition, available funds were insufficient to plan and implement outcome evaluations for all 20 projects. Consequently, the BASICS Management Board, staff, and research team jointly selected four projects for intensive outcome evaluations. These particular projects were selected based on the likelihood that the reform, if proven to be successful, could be instituted by other bar associations, organizations, or groups. These four projects were: (1) a prison legal services and paralegal training project in Michigan (Conner et al., 1978), (2) a citizen dispute settlement program in Florida (Conner and Surrette, 1977), (3) a jail legal services coordination project in Maryland (Huff, 1978a) and (4) an offender vocational training project, also in Maryland (Huff, 1978b).

Although the four projects employed different strategies of reform to attain their goals and were directed at diverse types of clients within the criminal justice system, there were similarities in the goals of each evaluation plan. First, the evaluations assessed the accuracy of the assumptions upon which each program was based. In two of the studies inmates were surveyed as to their perceptions of legal services, their need for a legal aid clinic, and their attitudes toward the criminal justice system. In a third study, citizens who participated in special dispute resolutions and a comparable group who did not have these hearings were asked about the outcomes of their disputes. In the fourth study, the assumptions underlying the reform (that is, vocational training for adult and juvenile offenders) were found to be inaccurate.

A second common goal among the studies was to assess the impact and effectiveness of each of the projects on their target group of clients. In the Florida project citizens made judgments about their degree of satisfaction with the settlements reached and about the likelihood that their complaints were resolved. In addition, the records of the state attorney's office were analyzed to assess the impact of these special hearings on the workload of that office. In the Montgomery County projects offenders who had been placed in jobs, following intensive training, were asked about their reactions to the program; in the Baltimore and

Michigan projects the types of legal services being rendered to inmates in two correctional facilities were assessed and the reactions of inmates and facility managers to these services were evaluated. In the Michigan project, the effectiveness of an inmate paralegal training program was also evaluated, using a control group design.

A third evaluation goal evident across all four of these projects was to assess the activity and involvement of members of the local bar association in the reform projects. To accomplish this, the evaluators gathered information regarding the number of attorneys who volunteered to work on the specific projects and the amount of other resources the local bar association contributed to each project.

DEVELOPING A MODEL FOR THE EVALUATOR-MANAGER RELATIONSHIP

As the descriptions of the planning and action phase evaluations demonstrate, the BASICS evaluation project involved many different evaluation and program personnel at many different levels. In spite of the large number and variety of relationships between evaluator and program personnel, there was little conflict. Although the evaluations were not always implemented as planned, the reasons for this did not relate to unsatisfactory evaluator-manager relations; rather, changed program circumstances necessitated revised evaluation plans.

Why was conflict a minor occurrence? Why were the many relationships between various evaluators and different program personnel characterized by trust and cooperation instead of suspicion and disagreement? The answer to the first question can be answered by analyzing the six sources of conflict, presented at the outset of this chapter, in relation to the BASICS evaluation program. The answer to the second question will be answered by explaining the model of the evaluator-manager relationship which guided the evaluation project.

The six sources of conflict described by Weiss (1972) were potentially present in the BASICS evaluation; however, little conflict occurred. The reasons for this varied for each potential conflict source.

(1) Personality differences. There were no significant personality differences among the evaluators and program personnel. Both of the primary evaluators had been involved previously in social reform work as program personnel. This previous experience may have made the evaluators more understanding of the program personnel's position. In addition, a large number of the people working on BASICS projects were lawyers, a professional group trained to be cool, rational thinkers. The similarity between a lawyer's training and that for an evaluator, whose scientific training is also very rational and logical, may be another factor which explains the absence of notable personality difference.

(2) Differences in roles. The BASICS evaluators and program personnel had different roles, a fact acknowledged by all parties. However, the difference in roles was not accentuated. The evaluators became de facto program personnel in terms of participation, working with the national and local projects from the outset and to a significant degree, just as other program staff would do. This willingness of the evaluators to become active, early, regular participants in program planning and implementation caused the apparent differences in role to be obscured, although the real difference remained. Indeed, the evaluators' regular participation made it possible for project staffs to learn about evaluation and facilitated their recognition, understanding, and acceptance of the necessary differences in role and expertise.

(3) Lack of clear role definition. This source of conflict was not present in the BASICS evaluations because in each case the evaluators and program staff reached a clear agreement, in writing, about the goals of the evaluation plan and the accompanying evaluation design, measures, and timetable. These agreements varied in their formality; several were in long letters detailing the aspects of the evaluation and others were more

formal evaluation proposals. This exercise helped to clarify at the outset the role requirements of each participant in the evaluation activities.

(4) Conflicting goals, values, interests, and frames of reference. At one level, the evaluators and program staffs had different goals: The evaluators were interested in assessment, the service providers were interested in service. At another level, however, the goals of the two groups were the same: to provide the best possible service to clients. The early and continued involvement of the evaluators with each project helped to convince the staff that the evaluators also were interested in good service delivery and that the skills of the evaluation researchers could be valuable to project staff in improving their provision of services. For example, the coordinator of the paralegal training program in the Michigan project was able to use pretest results on degree of legal knowledge among inmate trainers to select an appropriate beginning level for training. Similarly, the Baltimore project administrator was able to use survey results to identify problems in legal service coordination. In these cases, the utility of evaluation information for improving services became apparent to the staff, and this knowledge helped reduce apparent differences in interests and frames of reference.

(5) Institutional characteristics. These evaluation settings were *not* authoritarian, formal, and closed. On the contrary, the BASICS evaluation projects, by their very nature, involved a number of people with a variety of inputs on decisions for the projects. In all cases the evaluators worked closely with the main decision makers (managers, directors, and boards of control) and channels of communication were direct, two-sided, and always open.

(6) Aspects of evaluation methods and techniques. All the BASICS evaluation projects involved unusual, special evaluation techniques. At minimum, interviews and questionnaires were used with each project; in the Michigan project a control group was also used. These procedures generally did not present problems, in large part because they were instituted as a regular part

of the newly formed projects, not as special changes in well-established practices. Some of the evaluation procedures were welcomed by project staff. In the Michigan project, for example, where a control group was used, the random selection procedure was a boon to the training coordinator because he was able to assure the eligible but nonselected inmates that they had had an equal chance to be in the program and that favoritism had not played a part in selection.

A Collegial Model of Evaluator-Manager Relations

Many of these usual sources of conflict were not present in the BASICS evaluation project. In some cases this occurred because of special conditions of the BASICS Program. Institutional characteristics, for example, were not a source of conflict because of the new, demonstration-program nature of the correctional reform projects as well as the open, multiple-participant nature of the correctional reform effort. In other cases the conditions existed for these issues to become conflict sources (that is, differences in roles, lack of clear role definition, conflicting goals and frames of reference, and aspects of evaluation methods), but this generally did not occur. The reasons for the absence of conflict relates to the model which guided the evaluator-manager relationship.

At both the macrolevel—with the national BASICS Board of Directors and the BASICS program manager—and at the microlevel—with managers of the four individual projects—we used the same approach to the evaluator-manager relationship. The conceptual model which guided our activities consisted of four ordered parts (see Figure 1).

In the first stage, contact between the evaluator and other program staff occurs as soon as possible after the program is conceived so that everyone begins to work cooperatively as a team. The evaluator takes the lead in communicating a cooperative, collegial attitude toward the staff. These activities characterized the first stage of the contact of the evaluators

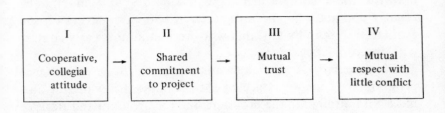

Figure 1: The Collegial Model of the Evaluator-Manager Relationship

with the BASICS program: the evaluators (1) began to work with the managers before the programs started; (2) quickly learned as much as they could about the programs; (3) planned the evaluation with the managers' help; and (4) presented and thoroughly discussed the final evaluation design, measures, and timetable with the managers.

The activities in Stage I produce a feeling of shared commitment to the project (Stage II). That is, the program manager begins to view the evaluator as another person involved in the reform effort rather than as an outsider or, in Weiss' terms, a "marginal man." In this stage the program staff begins to see that the evaluator is not present only to criticize the program, but instead to provide an objective assessment of the program's strengths and weaknesses. In addition, the staff begins to recognize advantages in the evaluation procedures and to see the utility, both short- and long-term, of the evaluation data. Both the evaluator and the program staff, then, begin to acknowledge the same general commitment to the reform effort while at the same time recognizing and understanding the differences in roles and behaviors.

In the BASICS Program this second stage was achieved when program staff began to ask the opinions of evaluators on decisions about program operation. The evaluators, in turn, consulted frequently with program staff in developing the final evaluation plans, particularly on the measures to be used and the procedures for administering the measures. In order to reaffirm their commitment, the evaluators also maintained regular contact with the programs, in two cases hiring on-site evaluation research assistants who were in almost daily contact with the projects.

These activities generated mutual trust (Stage III). Once program staff members accept the fact that the evaluator also has a commitment to the program, and the program and staff see indications that this commitment is genuine and long-term, they can begin to let down their guard and trust the evaluator. With this knowledge, the evaluator can trust the program staff, and can be assured inclusion in decisions on program changes and discussions of program operations. Without this mutual trust, there is always an unsettled, tentative quality to the evaluator-manager relationship.

In the BASICS Program the development of trust was facilitated by following up early collaboration in the evaluation planning with continued staff input into the evaluation process. For example, staff was promised copies of drafts of the interim and final evaluation reports. Their comments were solicited and they were assured that these comments would be included in the final versions of the reports. There was an unanticipated advantage to this procedure. In several instances program staff noted misstatements of facts which the evaluators were able to correct and so avoid potentially embarrassing errors in the final reports.

The last stage of the model is the mutual respect that characterizes a relationship with little conflict. The evaluator and program staff recognize and accept the differences in their tasks and jobs and are willing to defer on matters which relate directly to the evaluation or to the program. This last stage of mutual respect seemed to be reached with the National BASICS Management Board when the board devoted nearly one-fourth of its semiannual meeting to a thorough presentation and discussion of the findings from the first-year report (Huff et al., 1975), then accepted nearly all of the report recommendations.

The model presented here is conceptual, not empirically tested. Although based on qualitative judgments which were grounded in actual experiences, the model was not tested here. For example, changes in manager's degree of trust in the evaluators were not assessed. These kinds of changes could be researched, however, and the stages of the model could be put to a critical test.

CONCLUSIONS

This four-stage model of the evaluator-manager relationship emphasizes early, cooperative interaction between evaluators and program personnel. The program staff and the evaluator need to approach each other as equals in the reform process. There needs to be a mutual respect for the different skills each participant brings to the program and the different tasks each has to accomplish. Rather than highlighting the differences between the evaluator and the program staff, evaluators emphasize the similarities and take actions to minimize the differences where feasible, such as in learning more about the program, the community, the staff, and the managers; spending time experiencing the day-to-day activities of the program. By doing these things, evaluators earn the staffs' respect and the freedom to make decisions concerning the conduct of the evaluation, an area in which the staff has little expertise. For these reasons, the model is labeled the "collegial model."

There is, however, a potential danger for the evaluator in the collegial model. If the trust which develops between the evaluator and manager is more apparent than real on the part of the manager, the evaluator may be manipulated by the manager. The manager, for example, could try to steer the evaluator away from the assessment of certain program objectives or the reporting of certain unfavorable evaluation findings. There are two ways to avoid this danger: either by involving an independent critic at critical periods of the evaluation or through continuing personal awareness of the possibility. The former is unquestionably the more effective of these two strategies. In the case of the BASICS Program, these checks were provided by constant discussions between the two evaluation researchers. The activities of each of the evaluators in the planning phase were somewhat independent; during the action phase the evaluators worked completely independently. Consequently, the evaluators were able to serve as objective critics for each other.

The second strategy to avoid cooptation—concerted personal awareness—is less satisfactory because there is no outside, independent critic. This strategy involves ongoing self-evaluation, during which the evaluator must maintain a healthy skepticism about the *actual* reasons for different program decisions and program staff behaviors.

In the spirit of healthy skepticism, it is worth questioning whether this collegial model was really the cause of the cooperative relationship which results in the BASICS evaluation. Perhaps the approach was not the causal factor; this might have been one of those instances where—by chance—everything worked for the best. There are several reasons why we would doubt this.

First, in the five primary evaluator-manager relationships, there were varying degrees of cooperativeness. In those cases where evaluators experienced the best relationships with program personnel, the collegial model activities previously described were carried out to the fullest. Where the activities were not able to be carried out, the evaluator-manager relationship was less satisfactory. Stated in terms of the model, less cooperative interaction led to less shared commitment, which in turn created less mutual trust. This lack of mutual trust resulted in less respect and more conflict.

Second, the nonimplementation of certain evaluation activities was attributable more to the evaluators than to the managers. For example, one of the evaluators was unable to maintain close contact with a project due to illness; this affected the evaluation activities and, consequently, the quality of the relationship.

Third, in cases where conflict occurred, the reasons for this seemed to be unique and related to individual behaviors. For example, the evaluators had some conflict with a member of one project's advisory board. In spite of the attempts to work with this individual, he steadfastly refused to spend much time with the evaluators; consequently, important issues could not be resolved. The project staff had the same difficulty with him for essentially the same reason.

Fourth, the reform projects were very different. Yet, the evaluators were able to implement a suitable evaluation plan in spite of the many differences among project goals, clients, and personnel. These implementations of the collegial model could be viewed as independent replications of the efficacy of the model.

The collegial model, then, seems to have contributed greatly to the cooperative evaluator-manager relationships in the BASICS evaluations. In three instances, the relationship had a synergistic quality—improving the content of the program as well as the conduct of the evaluation. The improvement of the content of the programs occurred first via formative evaluation results presented and discussed with program staff, then later via the summative evaluation results. The conduct of the evaluation was improved because the program managers aided in the implementation of the evaluation. There was one unintended consequence of the evaluator-manager relationship which highlighted the extent to which the evaluations were accepted. After we were no longer associated with the individual projects, three of the four projects implemented the same evaluation plan for a second year, including, in one case, a control-group research design. This kind of unobtrusive measure of manager satisfaction with the evaluation provides additional support for the efficacy of a collegial evaluator-manager relationship.

NOTE

1. "Manager," "director," "practitioner," "staff," and "service provider" will be used interchangeably here to refer to program personnel in general. Although the types of relationships and, hence, the types of conflicts between evaluators and these various program personnel may differ to some extent, the similarities among the program personnel in regard to the evaluator are great enough to treat them as a group for the purposes of this discussion.

REFERENCES

ARGYRIS, C. (1971) "Creating effective research relationships in organizations." In F. G. Caro (ed.), Readings in Evaluation Research. New York: Russell Sage Foundation.

BASICS Program (1974) Information Brochure. Washington, DC: American Bar Association.

CONNER, R. F. and R. SURETTE (1977) The citizen Dispute Settlement Program: Resolving Disputes Outside the Court—Orlando, Florida. Washington, DC: American Bar Association.

CONNER, R. F., J. EMSHOFF, and W. DAVIDSON (1978) Legal Aid and Legal Education for Prisoners: An Evaluation of the State Bar of Michigan's Prison Project. Washington, DC: American Bar Association.

HUFF, C. R. (1978a) The Baltimore Jail Project: An Experiment in the Coordination of Legal Services. Washington, DC: American Bar Association.

——— (1978b) Correctional Reform through Vocational Training: An Assessment of the Montgomery County (Maryland) BASICS Project. Washington, DC: American Bar Association.

———, R. F. CONNER, and G. GEIS (1975) Planning Correctional Reform: An Assessment of the American Bar Association's BASICS Program. Washington, DC: American Bar Association.

RODMAN, H. and R. KOLODNY (1971) "Organizational strains in the researcher-practitioner relationship." In F. G. Caro (ed.) Readings in Evaluation Research. New York: Russell Sage Foundation.

WEISS, C. H. (1977) "Between the cup and the lip." In F. G. Caro (ed.) Readings in Evaluation Research. New York: Russell Sage Foundation.

——— (1975) "Evaluation research in the political context." In E. L. Struening and M. Guttentag (eds.) Handbook of Evaluation Research (Vol. 1). Beverly Hills, CA: Sage.

——— (1972) Evaluation Research: Methods of Assessing Program Effectiveness. Englewood Cliffs, NJ: Prentice-Hall.

Edward C. Weeks
*School of Community Service
and Public Affairs,
University of Oregon*

THE MANAGERIAL USE
OF EVALUATION FINDINGS

Social scientists are being called upon increasingly to use their methodological skills to identify and measure the consequences of social action programs. At both the federal and state levels, legislation in such areas as housing, community development, education, mental health, criminal justice, and medical services has included provisions requiring program evaluation.[1] An underlying assumption of these mandates is that evaluation will improve the effectiveness of social programs by providing program managers with information describing program performance.

While it would be most desirable to assess evaluations against the contribution they make to improved decision-making, discussions of the usefulness of evaluations generally have addressed the simpler question of utilization. The research reported here follows this tradition and examines the degree to which evaluations are used by managers of human service programs in making program decisions.

AUTHOR'S NOTE: *This chapter is a revised version of a paper presented at the annual meeting of the Evaluation Research Society, Washington, D.C., November 2-4, 1978.*

Despite Carol Weiss' call of a decade ago for the comparative study of evaluation utilization (1966), few empirical studies have been reported. There have been only two important studies focusing specifically on the utilization of evaluation findings (Patton et al., 1977; Alkin et al., 1974). Studies regarding the use of applied social research are somewhat more numerous (Weiss, 1977; Rich 1976; Caplan, 1976, 1977a, 1977b; Van de Vall and Bolas, 1977; Van de Vall et al., 1976; Lehne and Fisk, 1974).

In contrast to this dearth of empirical research on the use of evaluation findings in program decision-making is an abundance of nonempirical literature on this topic. This literature consists mainly of reflections or speculations by academics or practitioners on why evaluations are seldom used. Typically, each paper posits a potpourri of factors that are assumed to exert an important influence on the use of evaluation findings by decision makers (for a review of this literature, see Goldstein et al., 1978; and Cohen, 1977).

Reviewing the literature on evaluation utilization reveals three major themes which seem to tie together the large number of impediments to utilization suggested by other writers. These themes, or underlying factors, are: (1) the organizational location of the evaluator—specifically, the character and degree of interaction between the evaluator and the program personnel; (2) the methodological practices employed in performing the evaluation; and (3) the decision-making context. These three factors are the major independent—or, more accurately, predictor—variables of the research reported here. The remainder of this Chapter will be concerned with the more complete definition of these factors, their measurement, and the observed relationship of these factors to evaluation utilization. To set the stage for this discussion, however, it is first necessary to describe the dependent variable—utilization—and the level of program decision-making at which evaluation utilization is to be examined.

Rich (1976) has provided a useful discrimination between two broad categories of utilization: "conceptual," which refers to the cumulative influence of evaluation findings in shaping the thinking in a specific problem area; and "instrumental" utilization, which refers to the direct application of evaluation to a specific policy or decision. Consistent with the setting for this research, the emphasis here is on instrumental utilization—that is, the relatively short-term and direct application of evaluation findings to specific program decisions.

The implementation of social programs typically proceeds through a series of delegated responsibilities to smaller and smaller governmental or quasi-governmental units, ending at the local agency or project level where direct services are provided to intended recipients. The decisions made at this level determine what services are provided to whom, by whom, and the manner in which the services are provided. At this local level the three factors—organizational location of the evaluator, methodological practices, and decision context—are thought to influence the degree to which evaluation findings are applied to specific program decisions.

Organizational Location

There are three ways in which the evaluator's location is thought to influence the utilization of the evaluation findings.

(1) Through access to program decision makers. By having access to program decision makers, the evaluator is more likely to (a) be aware of the issues in which decision makers are interested, (b) possess greater authority to impose and enforce the requirements of a rigorous research design, and (c) participate to a greater degree in the decision-making process.

(2) Through knowledge about the program. By having knowledge of the program at its basic level of operation, the evaluator may have a better understanding of what changes are feasible and what implementation strategies would be most effective.

(3) Through the quality of the staff-evaluator relationship. An evaluator who is close to the operating level of the program is more likely to (a) minimize the staff's perception of the evaluation as a threat, (b) reduce the likelihood that staff will sabotage the

evaluation process, and (c) lessen the staff's opposition to the findings of the evaluation.

Methodological Practices

Program evaluation is primarily the application of social scientific methodologies to identify and measure the consequences of social action programs. The impact of an evaluation on agency decision-making depends in part on the adequacy of its methodology. The methodological practices employed in an evaluation may affect evaluation utilization in three major ways.

(1) Through the quality of the information provided. Decision makers will be most willing to use information that they consider valid, reliable, and rigorous. Experimental designs are considered more rigorous than quasi-experimental designs, with the latter being preferable to preexperimental designs.

(2) Through the amount of relevant information provided. Decision makers require information about program achievements toward a variety of goals and advice about specific operational changes in their programs. Evaluations conducted as true experiments may sacrifice the relevance of the information to decision makers for the rigor of design (Schulberg and Baker, 1968). Critics of the use of experimental designs point out that programs have multiple goals and comprise a complex set of interlocking activities. Experimental evaluations focus on a narrow set of goals and provide information about relative goal attainment, not the enhancement of goal attainment (Nielsen, 1975). Different methodologies have been suggested as more appropriate to the task of producing decision-relevant information. These methodologies generally call for an examination of the program-operating characteristics, attention to a variety of organizational goals and politics, and the frequent use of qualitative description.

(3) Through the organizational stress created in implementing the methodology. Evaluation methodologies vary in their obtrusiveness. An evaluation using an experimental design necessarily includes the random assignment of subjects (for example, indi-

viduals, schools, or communities) to treatment conditions. Further, an experimental design generally requires programs to remain fixed during the evaluation period. These requirements intrude on the prerogatives of management and practitioners and can sometimes create resistances or hostilities that carry over to the utilization process. Other methodological practices, such as the use of the program staff to collect data, the determination of effectiveness criteria, or the quantification of treatment and outcome variables, also can create strained relations between evaluator and program staff that would jeopardize utilization.

Decision Context

It is posited that there are also certain types of decision settings in which the information yielded by program evaluations will be most useful.

(1) The decisions have broad implications for and are important to the organization. In the language of Katz and Kahn (1966), the decisions are expected to (a) have a high level of generality, (b) affect a large amount of organizational space, and (c) be in effect for a long period of time. The decisions often will include the determination of general strategies for attaining organizational goals.

(2) There is difficulty in selecting alternative courses of action. This conceptualization of the decision-making process relies on March and Simon's (1958) characterization of the resolution strategies employed by individuals or groups experiencing a decision problem. They describe four processes through which organizations react to conflict: (a) problem-solving, (b) persuasion, (c) bargaining, and (d) "politics." The first two categories call for analytic strategies; the latter two call forth bargaining strategies. Analytic strategies are evoked when there is relative agreement about organizational goals and when the decision problem is to identify a solution that satisfies the shared criteria. Bargaining strategies are evoked when there is an absence of agreement on decision criteria; these are characterized by

acknowledged conflict of interest, gamesmanship, and the recruitment of allies.

Evaluation information is expected to be used most often in problem-solving or persuasion settings and less frequently in bargaining or "political" settings. By definition, problem-solving and persuasion modes of conflict resolution place a premium on assembling information and using that information to guide the problem-solving or persuasion process. The bargaining and "politics" modes of conflict resolution are power-oriented rather than information-oriented. Because the decision objectives are not shared, resolution depends more on the relative strength of the participants to decide which objectives are pursued and how they are pursued.

METHODOLOGY

To ascertain the relationships among these three factors— organizational location, methodological practices, and decision context—and the utilization of evaluation findings, the following study was conducted.

Subjects

Identified were 114 evaluations of social programs implemented at the local level in California from 1975 to 1977. Of these, 76 met the minimal criterion that the evaluation represent a systematic effort to identify and measure the consequences of the program. This criterion eliminated evaluations consisting solely of statements by the program personnel that the program was effective and evaluations consisting of simple counts of the units of service provided or the number of people served. Additionally, the person who had primary responsibility for the conduct of the evaluation had to be accessible.

Procedure

Following initial telephone contact, questionnaires were sent to the 76 evaluators. Of the questionnaires sent out, 57 (75 percent) were returned and analyzed. While the evaluated programs represented a wide range of human service programs, programs in the mental health (19 percent) and criminal justice (40 percent) areas predominated. In terms of the number of staff members in each program, 44 percent of the programs had less than 10 staff members, 30 percent had between 11 and 50 staff members and 26 percent of the programs had more than 50 staff members. The evaluation "teams" most frequently included only one person and seldom more than four. Finally, 24 percent of the programs in this sample employed major professionals, 28 percent employed minor professionals, 35 percent employed semiprofessionals, and 12 percent employed nonprofessionals as service providers.

Independent Variables

The *organizational location* of the evaluator was measured through an index composed of five elements:

(1) the frequency of meetings between program personnel and evaluators during the evaluation planning phase;
(2) the frequency of meetings between program personnel and evaluators for the purpose of data collection;
(3) the frequency of program management/evaluator meetings during the conduct of the evaluation;
(4) the decision-making relationship between the evaluation team and the program in determining the conduct of the evaluation (Did the evaluator have independence? independence with program review? Was decision-making shared with the program, or did the program personnel supervise the evalution?); and
(5) whether the program staff was given the opportunity to review and comment on the evaluation report prior to final submission.

In forming the organizational location index, the items were rescaled to contribute equal weights to the index. This practice was repeated for the methodological practices and decision context indices.

The index used to measure the *methodological practices* factor was composed of seven elements:

(1) the research design employed (experimental, quasi-experimental, nonexperimental with more than two measurement points, nonexperimental with two measurement points, nonexperimental with a single measurement point);
(2) sampling procedures (probability, systematic, accidental);
(3) the number of data collection methods used;
(4) the number of data sources used (clients, practitioners, other community members);
(5) the number of measures taken (the number of unique method-source pairs);
(6) instrumentation (the degree of structure and standardization present in the measurement instrument or procedure—from participant observation to standardized tests); and
(7) data analysis (the statistical complexity of data analysis procedures—from multivariate statistical analysis to narrative descriptive reports);

The index used to measure the *decision context* factor was composed of six elements. These elements and their rationale are described below.

(1) Number of decision participants. The rationale for this indicator is simply that as the number of participants increases, there is an associated increased likelihood of disagreement over the decision criteria. That is, it is thought to be easier to obtain consensus between two individuals than it is to obtain consensus among three, and so on.
(2) Specificity of program goals. Ambiguity of organizational objectives often masks disagreement over their acceptance. Where objectives are ambiguous, the decision-making process is more likely to be characterized by bargaining and politics.
(3) Professional status of practitioners. Where service deliverers have a strong professional identity, they are likely to demand a

role in organizational decision-making and are likely to share professional goals in addition to, or rather than, the organizational goals. The stronger the professional identity, the more likely that the decision-making process will be characterized by bargaining and politics.

(4) The number of program goals. Agencies often (perhaps always) have multiple goals. Individuals are likely to differ over the priority of the goals. The larger the number of goals, the more likely that differences in priority will emerge in the decision-making process, and the more likely that process will be characterized by bargaining and politics.

(5) Consistency of program goals. Where programs have multiple goals and when these goals are inconsistent with each other, conflict is likely to arise over which multiple goals will be favored. Two goals are considered consistent with each other if efforts to achieve one contribute to the achievement of the other.

(6) Existence of organized constituencies. Organized constituencies generally are concerned with a narrower set of agency objectives than are either line personnel or agency administrators. Further, their influence is generally exerted through political strategies rather than analytical strategies. For this research, the existence of organized constituency groups is thought to increase the likelihood of conflicting decision criteria and of bargaining and political decision strategies.

Dependent Variables

The dependent variable, utilization, was assessed on an instrument which presented ten statements describing varying degrees to which evelution findings were applied to specific program decisions. This instrument is presented in Figure 1.

The final statements used on the instrument were drawn from a larger pool of items after all items had been ranked by a small number of program evaluators and program managers. Subsequently, the statements contained in the scale were duplicated on small cards and sent to 63 program managers with instructions to rank-order the statements. Fifty-four completed rank-orderings were received and the percentage of agreement on the rank-order

41.   Are you familiar with the degree of utilization the evaluation received?
      (43)

      _____ *1 Yes, I have first-hand knowledge of how the findings were used.*
      _____ *2 Yes, I received reports from others about how the findings were used.*
      _____ *3 No.*

      If yes, which of the following statements best describes the degree to
      which the evaluation findings and recommendations were used in making
      program decisions? (The term "decision participants" is used to describe
      those individuals who actively participated in the formulation of program
      decisions; it may include those without formal decision-making authority.)
      (44)

      _____ 01 *Most of the decision participants probably didn't even read the
      report. Nobody considered that it could tell them much they
      didn't already know.*
      _____ 02 *The decision participants all looked at it, but I don't think it
      changed anyone's thinking.*
      _____ 03 *The decision participants thought the evaluation report pre-
      sented some interesting ideas, but I don't think it had any
      direct effect.*
      _____ 04 *The decision participants used the report as a starting point
      to discuss the issues. As far as the decisions that were actually
      made, I don't think the evaluation study contributed much.*
      _____ 05 *The decision participants discussed the findings and from that
      the decisions emerged. It's hard to trace the evaluation's exact
      role, but it definitely had some impact on the decisions.*
      _____ 06 *The evaluation study definitely had a major impact in indicat-
      ing to the decision participants what needed improvement, but
      the study was not used significantly in deciding how to achieve
      improvement.*
      _____ 07 *The evaluation results were an important, but not the most im-
      portant, source of information used by the decision participants
      in reaching decisions about the program.*
      _____ 08 *The evaluation report was probably the single most important
      piece of information the decision participants used. It was very
      instrumental in reaching decisions about the program.*
      _____ 09 *Several of the recommendations presented in the evaluation
      report were adopted in some slightly modified form. The evalu-
      ation findings set the general direction for program changes.*
      _____ 10 *Many of the recommendations were adopted and implemented.
      In that sense, the evaluation study effectively made the pro-
      gram decisions.*

Figure 1: Utilization

of each statement was calculated. The percentage of agreement for each statement ranged from a high of 94 percent to a low of 66 percent. Finally, the reliability of the scale was tested through a test-retest approach using a parallel form. The retest form, mailed to a subsample of respondents, contained the same basic statements worded in a more terse, more direct fashion. The zero-order correlation between the two forms was .84 ($n = 21$).

Limitations of This Study

There are two important limitations to this study. The first is the use of a self-administered survey method to investigate the highly complex, little-understood process of utilization. The increase in sample size and the standardization of measurement achieved through using a survey method required sacrificing the benefit of a richly textured data base possible through in-depth interviews. While the survey instrument has been extensively pretested, important contextual data nevertheless are lost through such an approach.

The second important limitation occurs through asking evaluators to rate the utilization their products received. While precautions were taken to assess whether the evaluators were familiar with the degree of utilization the evaluation received, the threat of a systematic response bias exaggerating the degree of utilization could not be examined.

Results and Discussion

The first important finding is that at the local level evaluations appear to be generally well utilized (Table 1). Slightly more than 50% of the respondents reported that the evaluation report was an important source of information used by decision makers in reaching decisions about the program.

This finding contrasts with a large body of literature asserting that evaluations are seldom used. The apparent contradiction between the present finding of at least a moderate level of utilization and conventional wisdom is probably due to the different

Table 1: Degree of Utilization

Value	Brief Label[a]	Frequency	Percentage
1	Report not read	3	5.3
2	Changed no one's thinking	5	8.7
3	Interesting ideas but no effect	4	7.1
4	Starting point to discuss issues	5	8.7
5	Decisions emerged from discussion but report did not contribute much	5	8.7
6	Used to identify problems; not used to decide action	5	8.7
7	Important but not most important information	9	15.7
8	Most important information	4	7.1
9	Recommendations adopted in slightly modified form	11	19.3
10	Recommendations adopted and implemented	6	10.5
	TOTAL	57	100.0

a. See Figure 1 for complete description of response categories.

levels of analysis underlying these statements. To the degree that statements of nonutilization refer to utilization at high policy levels, the statements very well may be correct (see, for example, Rich, 1977), while the findings reported here are in reference to "lower," more operation-oriented levels of decision-making. It seems reasonable to expect that decision-making at high policy levels would concern broader issues and would take place in an environment where there are a greater number of competing interests and a wider range of information sources and where the evaluation report is less likely to present clear, action-relevant findings. Wholey (1972), commenting on the differences between the two broad levels of decision-making, concluded:

Over the past two years, members of the evaluation group at the Urban Institute have become more and more convinced that the primary evaluation payoff (in terms of decisions actually influenced) may be in evaluation that is done is sufficient detail to get at effects of operational changes within operating programs [Wholey, 1972: 265].

The findings reported here seem to support this position.

The observed relationship between the *organizational location* of the evaluator and evaluation utilization is extremely weak, both for the five items making up the index and for the index itself (Table 2): All rank-order correlation coefficients were less than −.18. The only component that even approaches significance is the evaluation decision-making relationship, suggesting that the greater the role of program personnel in shaping the evaluation, the more likely it is that the results will be used. This relationship is very slight, however, and probably should be considered a chance finding.

The observed relationship between *methodological practices* and evaluation utilization is much stronger (Table 3). Five of the seven components making up the index show correlations of sufficient magnitude to be considered nonchance findings, had the sample been randomly drawn, with correlation coefficients ranging from .19 to .31.

Research design—measured ordinally as experimental, quasi-experimental, nonexperimental with multiple measurement points, and nonexperimental with a single measurement point, in decreasing rank order—is negatively correlated with· utilization (Spearman's rho = −.24, $p < .05$). While this finding may be rejected as a chance finding, the pattern of relationships across the other dimensions of methodological practice and the findings of other researchers suggest that this finding reflects a real relationship.

The pattern of correlation between specific methodological features and evaluation utilization suggests that decision makers are, in fact, sensitive to the methodological basis of the evaluation findings. It is clear, for example, that they prefer evaluations employing multiple measures (Spearman's rho = .31) taken from

**Table 2: Relationship Between Organizational Location
of Evaluator and Utilization**

	Spearman's rho
Frequency of program/evaluator meetings —evaluation planning phase	.06
Frequency of program/evaluator meetings —for purposes of data collection	−.01
Frequency of management/evaluator meetings —for purposes other than data collection	−.04
Evaluation decision-making relationship	−.18
Program review of evaluation report	−.02

Combined Index
Pearson r = −.03

multiple sources (Spearman's rho = .23), and that they appreciate —at least intuitively—problems of sampling bias (Spearman's rho = .26). The findings here suggest that decision makers are less influenced by the degree of standardization present in the measurement process (Spearman's rho = .19) and that they may have a slight preference for the more qualitative forms of data analysis (Spearman's rho = −.17).

When the direction of the relationships is examined, the findings of this research again appear to contradict conventional wisdom on the role of specific methodological practices in evaluation utilization. This "conventional wisdom" is reflected in a statement by Rossi and Wright (1977): "There is almost universal agreement among evaluation researchers that the randomized controlled experiment is the ideal model for evaluating the effectiveness of a public policy" (1977: 13), although the proliferation of experimental designs in public program evaluation "is nowhere supported by empirical confirmation of their superiority in planned social intervention" (Van de Vall and Bolas, 1977: 1).

Van de Vall and Bolas (1977), in investigating the policy impact of applied social research, examined the influence of research methodology along a dimension they termed "scope"—defined as the number and diversity of variables encompassed by a re-

Table 3: Relationship Between Methodological Practices
and Utilization

Methodological Feature	Spearman's rho	Pearson r
Design	−.24[a]	−.23[a]
Sampling	.26[a]	.30[a]
Number of data-collection methods	.31[a]	.30[a]
Number of measures taken	.31[a]	.31[a]
Number of data sources	.23[a]	.23[a]
Instrumentation	.19	.19
Data analysis	−.15	−.17

Combined Index
Pearson r = .20
a. $p < .05$.

search method. They developed the following classification of
methods:

> Narrow scope: laboratory experiments, field experiments, socio-
> metric analysis; medium scope: focused survey research, deviant
> case studies, observational methods, statistical trend analysis;
> and wide scope: comprehensive survey research, representative
> case studies, socio-historical analysis, qualitative data analysis
> [Van de Vall and Bolas, 1977: 3].

Comparing the scope of the research methods against the use
of the findings, Van de Vall and Bolas concluded that "the broader
the multivariate 'scope' of methods of social policy research, the
more intensively the methods are used for purposes of social
problem solving" (1977: 4). The pattern of relationships found
in the present research appears to corroborate Van de Vall and
Bolas' findings.

The correlation between the separate methodological features
and utilization is suppressed slightly when combined to form the
methodological practice index (Pearson r = .20). It is interesting
to note, however, that the regression of utilization on the separate
items yields an adjusted multiple R^2 of .30. When the items are

Table 4: Relationship Between Decision Context Factors and Utilization

	Spearman's rho	Pearson r
Number of decision participants	n/a	.40[b]
Goal ambiguity—after evaluation	−.26[a]	−.24[a]
Professional status of program practitioner	−.04	−.06
Number of program goals	.09	.04
Consistency of organizational goals	−.10	−.18
Organized program constituency	−.02	.00

Combined Index
Pearson r = −.07
a. $p < .05$.
b. $p < .001$.

included in a stepwise fashion, the number of data-collection methods, the research design, and the sampling procedures account for 22 percent (adjusted) of the variance (F = 5.19, $p < .01$).

There is no observed relationship between the *decision context* index and evaluation utilization (r = .07; see Table 4). Of the items included in the decision context index, the number of decision participants shows the strongest relationship (r = .40, $p < .001$), but in a direction opposite that expected. Of the remaining items, only the specificity of program goals shows a significant relationship (rho = -.26, $p < .05$) which, additionally, is in the expected direction.

A post hoc explanation for the strong positive relationship observed between the number of people participating in decisions following the submission of the evaluation report and the use of the evaluation findings in making program decisions is that the number of participants reflects the importance assigned to the evaluation. That is, if the evaluation report is perceived as an important document, more people are likely to make an effort to participate in its discussion and in the decisions which follow. Further, participation may lessen resistance to using the evaluation findings which would serve to increase the use the findings received.

It is difficult to interpret the meaning of the negative correlation (Spearman's rho = -.26 p <.05) between goal specificity and utilization. It was hypothesized that where goals are vague, decision-making is more likely to be characterized by bargining, which, in turn, would lessen the importance of empirically derived information. The pattern of extremely low correlations for the other items in the decision context factor call into question the plausibility of this interpretation and suggest that the observed relationship is due to some unique relationship (not related to the general factor of decision context) between goal specificity and utilization.

CONCLUSION

It was suggested that the instrumental utilization of evaluation findings in program decision-making at the operational level could be understood through reference to three key factors: organizational location, methodological practices, and decision context. The simple correlation between the indices of each of the factors and evaluation utilization is small: -.03 for the organizational location index, -.07 for the decision context index, and .20 for the methodological practices index. When the individual items are examined, the picture becomes a bit brighter, suggesting some important relationships among various aspects of methodology and utilization and perhaps for certain aspects of the decision context.

The central question at this point is whether to abandon the present conceptualization for a different one. It is clear that the continued production of lists of possible impediments to utilization is not going to shed much light on the dynamics of utilization. Instead, progress at this point likely will occur through synthesizing the multitude of impediments already suggested into a few general factors. The factors examined in this research have an appealing internal logic and, for this writer, continue to hold promise. What is needed is more and better research on evaluation utilization, especially at the service delivery level, where systematic evaluation may offer the greatest benefit.

NOTE

1. See, for example, 42 USC § 5305 (Housing and Community Development); 42 USC § 2992 (Community Economic Development); 42 USC § 2928m and 42 USC § 2929C (Early Childhood Education); 42 USC § 2689 (c) (Community Mental Health); 42 USC § 3885 (Juvenile Delinquency Prevention and Control); 42 USC § 3742 (National Institute of Law Enforcement and Criminal Justice); 42 USC § 2689g(a) (National Center for the Prevention and Control of Rape); 42 USC § 242g (National Health Planning and Development Act); 42 USC § 2932 (Day Care Centers); 42 USC § 2572(g) (Manpower Development).

REFERENCES

ALKIN, M. C., S. KOSECOFF, C. FITZGIBBON, and R. SELIGMEN (1974) Evaluation and Decision Making: The Title VII Experience. CSE Monograph Series in Evaluation, No. 4. Los Angeles: Center for the Study of Evaluation, University of California.

CAPLAN, N. (1977a) "A minimal set of conditions necessary for the utilization of social science knowledge in policy formulation at the National level." In C. H. Weiss (ed.) Using Social Research in Public Policy Making. Lexington, MA: Lexington.

——— (1977b) "Social research and national policy: What gets used, by whom, for what purposes, and with what effect." In M. Guttentag (ed.) Evaluation Studies Review Annual (Vol. 2). Beverly Hills, CA: Sage.

——— (1976) "Factors associated with knowledge use among federal executives." Policy Studies 4:229-234.

CARO, F. G. [ed.] (1971) Readings in Evaluation Research. New York: Russell Sage Foundation.

COHEN, L. H. (1977) "Factors affecting the utilization of mental health evaluation research findings." Professional Psychology 8:526-534.

GOLDSTEIN, M. S., A. C. MARCUS, and N. P. RAUSCH (1978) "The nonutilization of evaluation research." Pacific Sociological Review 21:21-38.

KATZ, D. and R. KAHN (1966) The Social Psychology of Organizations. New York: John Wiley.

LEHNE, R. and D. M. FISK (1974) "The impact of urban policy analysis." Urban Affairs Quarterly 10:115-139.

NIELSEN, V. G. (1975) "Why evaluation does not improve program effectiveness." Policy Studies 3:385-397.

PATTON, M. Q., P. S. GRIMES, K. GUTHRIE, N. J. BRENNAN, B. D. FRENCH, and D. A. BLYTH (1977) "In search of impact: An analysis of the utilization of federal health evaluation research." In C. H. Weiss (ed.) Using Social Research in Public Policy Making. Lexington, MA: Lexington.

RICH, R. F. (1976) "Uses of social science information by federal bureaucrats: Knowledge for action versus knowledge for understanding." Presented at the 1976 Annual Meeting of the Midwest Political Science Association, Chicago, Illinois, April 29-May 1.

ROSSI, P. H. and S. R. WRIGHT (1977) "Evaluation research: An assessment of theory, practice and politics." Evaluation Quarterly 1:5-51.

SCHULBERG, M. C. and F. BAKER (1968) "Program evaluation models and the implementation of research findings." American Journal of Public Health 58:1248-1255.

SCRIVEN, M. (1976) "Payoffs from evaluation," in C. C. Abt (ed.) The Evaluation of Social Programs. Beverly Hills, CA: Sage.

VAN DE VALL, and C. BOLAS (1977) "Policy research as an agent of planned social intervention: An evaluation of methods, standards, data and analytic techniques." Presented at the Annual Convention of the American Sociological Association, Chicago, September 5-9.

——— and T. S. KANG (1976) "Applied social research in industrial organizations: An evaluation of function, theory, and methods." Journal of Applied Behavioral Science 12:158-177.

WEISS, C. H. (1966) "Utilization of evaluation: Toward comparative study." Presented at the Annual Meeting of the American Sociological Association, Miami Beach, Florida, September 1.

——— and M. J. BUCUVALAS (1977) "The challenge of social research to decision making." In C. H. Weiss (ed.) Using Social Research in Public Policy Making. Lexington, MA: Lexington.

WHOLEY, J. S. (1972) "What can we actually get from program evaluation?" Policy Sciences 3:361-369.

ABOUT THE CONTRIBUTORS

ANTHONY BROSKOWSKI received his Ph.D. in clinical psychology in 1967. He has served on the faculty of the University of Pittsburgh and the Harvard Medical School, Laboratory of Community of Community Psychiatry. His most recent publications are in the areas of program evaluation and management information systems. He has served as a planner and consultant for state and federal government agencies and is currently the Executive Director of the Northside Community Mental Health Center in Tampa, Florida.

RAYMOND W. CARLSON is Associate Professor at the Maritime School of Social Work, Dalhousie University, Halifax, Nova Scotia. He is a cofounder of the Maritime Evaluation Research Training Institute and is involved with several research and planning projects in a variety of human service fields. His emphasis is on defining and measuring service outcomes with a prioritization on utilization. He received his Ph.D. from the School of Social Work and served on the faculty of that school for several years. He was also a senior research associate at the Human Services Institute of Montgomery County, Pennsylvania.

ROSS F. CONNER is Assistant Professor in the Program in Social Ecology and Research Psychologist in the Public Policy Research Organization, both at the University of California, Irvine. He is the coauthor of *Sesame Street Revisited* (Russell Sage Foundation, 1975) and *Attorneys as Activists: Evaluating the American Bar Association's BASICS Programs* (1979, Sage Publications). In addition, Dr. Conner has written a number of papers on evaluation research. His current work focuses on the ethics of using control-group research designs in evaluation projects, as well as on the evaluation of research utilization.

JEANETTE M. JERRELL is Assistant Professor of Clinical Psychiatry at the University of Pittsburgh School of Medicine and Coordinator of Regional Education, Office of Education and Regional Programming at Western Psychiatric Institute and Clinic. She has served as an evaluator on several educational, mental health, and management training projects.

PATRICK LARKEY is Assistant Professor of Social Science and Public Policy at Carnegie-Mellon University. He is the author of *Evaluating Public Programs: The Impact of Revenue Sharing on Municipal Governments* (Princeton University Press, 1979).

RICHARD H. LONGABAUGH received his Ed.D. in human development from Harvard University in 1962. After several academic positions and a one-year postdoctoral fellowship in clinical psychology at the Langley Porter Neuropsychiatric Institute of the University of California, he moved to his current positions as Director of the Evaluation Division at Butler Hospital and Professor of Psychiatry and Human Behavior at Brown University. His research interests include mental health evaluation research and use of the problem-oriented system of treatment.

DWIGHT N. McNEILL received his M.P.H. in chronic disease epidemiology from Yale University in 1973. He was an NIMH Research Fellow in psychiatric epidemiology at the Psychiatric Epidemiology Research Unit affiliated with Columbia University. Currently, he is Senior Program Evaluator at Butler Hospital. His research interests include evaluation of mental health and alcoholism programs, the application of epidemiologic techniques in program evaluation, and the effect of reimbursement policies on the provision of services.

JONATHAN A. MORELL is Assistant Professor in the Hahnemann Department of Mental Health Sciences at the Hahnemann Medical College and Hospital of Philadelphia. He is coeditor of the journal *Evaluation and Program Planning*. Dr. Morell is the author of numerous articles on evaluation and is currently working on a book (tentatively titled *Program Evaluation in Social Research*).

HERBERT C. SCHULBERG is Professor of Clinical Psychiatry and Psychology, University of Pittsburgh School of Medicine, and Director of the Office of Education and Regional Programming at Western Psychiatric Institute and Clinic. The planning and evaluation of human service programs are the focus of his activities and numerous publications.

PAUL E. SPECTOR received his Ph.D. in industrial organizational psychology from the University of South Florida. He has taught business management at that school and currently holds a faculty appointment in the Department of Psychology. Dr. Spector's publications have been in the areas of organizational behavior, multivariate data analysis, and small group behavior. He is currently Director of Program Planning and Evaluation at Northside Community Mental Health Center, Tampa, Florida.

LEE SPROULL is Assistant Professor of Social Science at Carnegie-Mellon University. She is the coauthor (with Stephen Weiner and David Wolf) of *Organizing an Anarchy: Belief, Bureaucracy, and Politics in the National Institute of Education* (University of Chicago Press, 1978).

JOHN F. STEVENSON received his Ph.D. in psychology from the University of Michigan in 1973. He is currently employed at the University of Rhode Island. Dr. Stevenson's research interests include mental health evaluation research, cognitive personality variables, and the effects of environmental stress—in interaction with individual differences—on coping behavior.

EDWARD C. WEEKS is Assistant Professor of Public Affairs at the University of Oregon. His research is concerned with the application of social science knowledge and methods to the formation of public policy.

STEPHEN L. WHITE is Deputy Director at Northside Community Mental Health Center in Tampa, Florida, and Instructor of Psychiatry at the University of South Florida College of Medicine. His formal training is in the fields of clinical social work and health services administration. Mr. White has published in the areas of family therapy and human services management and is currently preparing a book on middle management in the human services.

CHARLES WINDLE is Program Evaluation Specialist in the Mental Health Services Development Branch of the National Institute of Mental Health. His primary current interests include the developments of methods for program evaluation, substantive evaluation of the Community Mental Health Centers Program, and citizen participation in mental health services planning and evaluation. Dr. Windle has a Ph.D. in experimental psychology from Columbia University.